LiT LiBs

Mash Up
a Classic

This INSTANT BESTSELLER belongs to:

_____

POTTER STYLE

Design by Danielle Deschenes
Text by Patrick Baker

ISBN: 978-0-307-59090-9

DEAREST READER,

When I was first approached about writing a book, I decided it was time to finally write that Great American Novel that had been inside me for so many years. So, on my first day, I rose at the first light of dawn, made a cup of coffee, put a sheet of paper into my typewriter, and sat down. As I looked at that blank page, thinking of the journey that lay before me, a thought occurred to me that has struck every great writer before: Forget this; this crap is too hard.

So, a few days later, after sending off my manuscript, I received notes from the publisher ... this is unacceptable, this is a breach of contract, this is just *The Great Gatsby* with the title changed to *The Sound and the Fury* and your name at the bottom, blah blah blah. We've all heard this before. Publishers, am I right?

In the face of this dilemma, I was struck by genius. What if I just used half of the words from great books and then let someone else fill in the rest? When I mentioned this to my editors, I was given the go-ahead with an encouraging "fine, whatever." The rest, as they say, is history.

Allow me a few words on how best to appreciate my work of genius. I highly recommend playing with others, but of course you can play alone if you're socially inept or all your relations died in a mine collapse or something. Just fill in the blanks with the word or phrase requested, and then plug those words into the passage on the next page. I know you lack self control, but don't look at the passage first unless otherwise told to. If we wanted you to do that, we'd put the passage first, now, wouldn't we?

Please enjoy this book, and share it with your friends. But make them buy their own copy, OK? I'm putting a deck on my house, and the contractor is really taking me for a ride.

SINCERELY,

Wright N. Poorly

Wuthering Appalachian Heights

Wuthering Heights is one of the most romantic books ever written. Just imagine it: troubled lovers in the hills of England who can never make their love come to be. Of course, it becomes increasingly less romantic when you realize they were raised as brother and sister. It's even less romantic if the story takes place in the backwoods hills of the South and they actually are brother and sister. To hear the most romantic story ever told at an Appalachian family reunion, fill in the blanks.

A BIG CITY	1	_____
BODY PART	2	_____
A SOUTHERN STATE	3	_____
GROUP OF PEOPLE FROM BIG CITY IN #1	4	_____
A LOCATION IN A SMALL REDNECK TOWN	5	_____
A JUNK FOOD	6	_____
VERB (ENDING IN –ING)	7	_____
NOUN (PLURAL)	8	_____
INJURY	9	_____
ANOTHER INJURY	10	_____
AN UNCLE WITH A STRANGE NAME	11	_____
CITY FROM #1	12	_____
A COMMUNITY ORGANIZATION (THE KNIGHTS OF COLUMBUS, THE MINUTEMEN, THE NEIGHBORHOOD WATCH, ETC.)	13	_____
BACKWOODS-SOUNDING TOWN	14	_____
A COUSIN WITH A STRANGE NAME	15	_____
EMOTIONAL VERB (AROUSE, ENRAGE, SEDATE, ETC.)	16	_____
COUSIN FROM #15	17	_____
SYNONYM FOR "FAMILY"	18	_____
UNCLE FROM #11	19	_____
SOMETHING FROM A COUNTRY STORE	20	_____
SOMETHING ELSE FROM A COUNTRY STORE	21	_____
SOMETHING ELSE FROM A COUNTRY STORE	22	_____
SOMETHING ELSE FROM A COUNTRY STORE	23	_____

"This is nothing," cried she: "I was only going to say that

1_____ did not seem to be my home; and I broke my

2_____ with weeping to come back to 3_____;

and the 4_____ were so angry that they flung me out

into the middle of the 5_____ on top of [my]

6_____; where I woke 7_____ for

8_____. That will do to explain my 9_____,

as well as the 10_____. I've no more business to marry

11_____ than I have to be in 12_____;

and if the 13_____ in 14_____ had

not brought 15_____ so low, I shouldn't have thought of

it. It would 16_____ me to marry 17_____

now; so he shall never know how I love him: and that, not because

he's 18_____, Nelly, but because he's more myself than I

am. Whatever our souls are made of, his and mine are the same; and

19_____'s is as different as 20_____

from 21_____, or 22_____ from

23_____.

Edgar Allen Poe:
Terrible Coworker

You know that person at work? The obnoxious one? From a few cubicles over? Don't you just *hate* him? Sure, maybe you don't have a good reason. Maybe his laugh is annoying. Or he eats lunch a little too loudly. Or he always refers to Wednesday as "hump day." Whatever the reason, don't you just want to murder him, cut him up, put the severed pieces under your floorboards, and let the nonexistent sound of his heartbeat slowly drive you crazy? No? Oh well, maybe that's just me then ...

FILL IN THE BLANKS TO SEE WHAT WOULD HAPPEN IF
THE NARRATOR FROM POE'S "THE TELL-TALE HEART" HAD
TO SHARE AN OFFICE WITH YOUR ANNOYING COWORKER.

BODY PART	1	_____
SYNONYM FOR "TOLERATED" (ACCEPTED, PUT UP WITH, DEALT WITH, DIDN'T MIND, ETC.)	2	_____
OCCUPATION OF YOUR LAME OFFICE MATE	3	_____
VERB (OF AN INAPPROPRIATELY SEXUAL NATURE, PAST TENSE)	4	_____
A TERRIBLE SECRET SANTA GIFT (PLURAL)	5	_____
ITEM AT COWORKER'S DESK	6	_____
BODY PART	7	_____
BODY PART FROM #7 (PLURAL)	8	_____
ANIMAL	9	_____
UNATTRACTIVE ADJECTIVE	10	_____
ANNOYING FASHION ACCESSORY	11	_____
OCCUPATION FROM #3	12	_____
BODY PART FROM #7	13	_____

It is impossible to say how first the idea entered my 1_____,
but, once conceived, it haunted me day and night. Object there was none.
Passion there was none. I 2_____ the 3_____.
He had never 4_____ me. He had never given me
5_____. For his 6_____ I had no
desire. I think it was his 7_____! Yes, it was this! One of
his 8_____ resembled that of a 9_____—a
pale 10_____ eye with a 11_____ over it.
Whenever it fell upon me my blood ran cold, and so by degrees, very
gradually, I made up my mind to take the life of the 12_____,
and thus rid myself of the 13_____ for ever.

Alice in Fat Camp

Alice's Adventures in Wonderland is full of discussions on the nature of madness. But maybe the Mad Hatter should stop thinking about what's under his mercury-lined headpiece and more about what's inside his gut. Between the Mad Tea crumpets, the Queen's tarts, huge mushrooms, and poorly labeled things that just say "eat me," there are a lot of ways to pig out in Wonderland. Fill in the blanks to see what happens when Wonderland becomes less concerned with who's mad as who's carb-counting.

SYNONYM FOR "BIG"	1	_____
A FAT CELEBRITY	2	_____
ANOTHER FAT CELEBRITY	3	_____
VERB (A SLOTHFUL ACTIVITY, ENDING IN —ING)	4	_____
SYNONYM FOR "FAT"	5	_____
WORD FROM #5	6	_____
WORD FROM #5	7	_____
WORD FROM #5	8	_____
ANOTHER SYNONYM FOR "FAT"	9	_____
ANOTHER SYNONYM FOR "FAT"	10	_____
A TYPICALLY SKINNY PERSON	11	_____
ANOTHER SYNONYM FOR "FAT"	12	_____
WORD FROM #11	13	_____
VERB (A FORM OF EXERCISE, ENDING IN "S")	14	_____
SYNONYM FOR "HUNGRY"	15	_____
SYNONYM FOR "PURGES"	16	_____
SYNONYM FOR "FULL"	17	_____
SYNONYM FOR "EAT"	18	_____
WORD FROM #15	19	_____
SYNONYM FOR "OVEREATING"	20	_____
WORD FROM #17	21	_____
WORD FROM #5	22	_____
SYNONYM FOR "RELAXING"	23	_____
WORD FROM #20	24	_____

"In that direction," the Cat said, waving its 1_____ paw round, "lives 2_____: and in that direction," waving the other paw, "lives 3_____. Visit either you like: they're both 4_____."

"But I don't want to go among 5_____ people," Alice remarked.

"Oh, you can't help that," said the Cat: "we're all 6_____ here. I'm 7_____. You're 8_____."

"How do you know I'm 9_____?" said Alice.

"You must be," said the Cat, "or you wouldn't have come here."

Alice didn't think that proved it at all: however, she went on: "And how do you know that you're 10_____?"

"To begin with," said the Cat, "a 11_____'s not 12_____. You grant that?"

"I suppose so," said Alice.

"Well, then," the Cat went on, "you see a 13_____ 14_____ when it's 15_____, and 16_____ when it's 17_____. Now I 18_____ when I'm 19_____, and 20_____ when I'm 21_____. Therefore I'm 22_____."

"I call it 23_____ not 24_____," said Alice.

"Call it what you like," said the Cat.

She's a poet, but keeps a day job as a hermit

Oh, Emily Dickenson, you're so … special. For someone who spent most of her life in one room and spoke to visitors from the other side of the door, you sure wrote a lot of good poems. But prolific as you were, there's only so much inspiration that can come from four walls. See, some of your poems were, oh, let's just say it…. bad. Like teen-angst bad. Like local-emo-band bad. Like really-sad-and-reclusive-monkey-at-a-typewriter bad. You had 1,800 poems locked away in a chest, and some for good reason. Like this one …

ANIMAL	1	_____
TYPE OF PERSON IN YOUR NEIGHBORHOOD	2	_____
BRAND OF SODA	3	_____
ADJECTIVE	4	_____
VERB (PAST TENSE)	5	_____
BRAND OF CAR	6	_____
ADJECTIVE	7	_____
NOUN (PLURAL)	8	_____
ADJECTIVE	9	_____
TYPE OF CANDY BAR	10	_____
VERB (PAST TENSE)	11	_____
BODY PART ON ANIMAL FROM #1	12	_____
COLOR	13	_____
ANOTHER ANIMAL (PLURAL)	14	_____
VERB	15	_____

A 1_____ came down the walk:

He did not know I saw;

He bit an 2_____ in halves

And ate the fellow, raw.

And then he drank a 3_____

From a 4_____ grass,

And then 5_____ sidewise to the wall

To let a 6_____ pass.

He glanced with 7_____ eyes

That hurried all abroad,—

They looked like frightened 8_____, I thought;

He stirred his 9_____ head

Like one in danger; cautious,

I offered him a 10_____,

And he 11_____ his 12_____

And rowed him softer home

Than oars divide the ocean,

Too 13_____ for a seam,

Or 14_____, off banks of noon,

15_____, splashless, as they swim.

Call of the Wild
Municipal Dog Park

Without question, Buck from Jack London's *The Call of the Wild* is an
impressive dog. A dog who rises above his pampered roots to become the
most respected and feared creature in the wild. Odds are your dog is
nothing like this. Odds are your dog wouldn't know how to kill a can
of Alpo. Fill in the blanks here to find out what *The Call of the Wild*
would have been like if it starred your everyday suburban mutt.

ADVERB	1	_____
AREA IN THE BACKYARD	2	_____
SYNONYM FOR "ESSENCE" (AS IN "THE ESSENCE OF THE OCEAN")	3	_____
ITEM FOUND IN THE BACKYARD	4	_____
ADJECTIVE	5	_____
A SMALL, NOT VERY IMPRESSIVE CREATURE	6	_____
SYNONYM FOR "PRESENCE"	7	_____
ITEM FOUND IN THE BACKYARD	8	_____
PIECE OF JUNK LEFT AROUND THE HOUSE	9	_____
ADVERB	10	_____
ADVERB	11	_____
OCCUPATION	12	_____
CREATURE FROM #6 (PLURAL)	13	_____
EQUIVALENT OF HANDS FOR THESE CREATURES (PLURAL)	14	_____

All day Buck brooded by the pool or roamed 1_____ about
the 2_____. . . . At times when he paused to
contemplate the 3_____ of the 4_____,
he forgot the pain of it; and at such times he was aware of a great pride in
himself—a pride 5_____er than any he had yet experienced.
He had killed 6_____, the noblest game of all, and he had
killed in the 7_____ of the 8_____ and
9_____. He sniffed the bodies 10_____.
They had died so 11_____. It was harder to kill
a 12_____ than them. They were no match at all, were it
not for their arrows and spears and clubs. Thenceforward he would be
unafraid of 13_____ except when they bore in their
14_____ their arrows, spears, and clubs.

Michael Scott, I presume?

Think of Ricky Gervais's character from *The Office*. Got it? Okay, now think of Steve Carrell's character in *The Office*. Got it? Now think of your real boss who quotes *The Office* too much to prove that "he gets it, he's hip." Got it? Now imagine they have some sort of weird, three-way man-baby, and that baby grows up to be your boss at an outpost in the middle of the god-forsaken nowheres of Africa. Granted, the manager from *Heart of Darkness* wasn't quite that bad, but with just a few changes he could be. Fill in the blanks to experience the worst boss *ever*.

ADJECTIVE	1	_____
ADJECTIVE TO DESCRIBE A FARM ANIMAL	2	_____
ADJECTIVE	3	_____
UNUSUAL COLOR	4	_____
SEXUAL ADJECTIVE	5	_____
UNUSUAL ANIMAL	6	_____
SYNONYM FOR "FRIGHTEN"	7	_____
TYPE OF PERSON OR ANIMAL (PLURAL)	8	_____
BODY PART	9	_____
A GESTURE OR PHYSICAL TICK	10	_____
GESTURE FROM #10	11	_____
ADJECTIVE	12	_____
GESTURE FROM #10	13	_____
ADJECTIVE	14	_____
OCCUPATION	15	_____

"My first interview with the manager was 1_____. . . . He was 2_____ in complexion, in features, in manners, and in voice. He was of middle size and of 3_____ build. His eyes, of the usual 4_____, were perhaps remarkably 5_____, and he certainly could make his glance fall on one as trenchant and heavy as a(n) 6_____. But even at these times the rest of his person seemed to 7_____ the 8_____. Otherwise there was only an indefinable, faint expression of his 9_____, something stealthy—a 10_____—not a 11_____—I remember it, but I can't explain. It was 12_____, this 13_____ was though just after he had said something it got intensified for an instant. It came at the end of his speeches like a seal applied on the words to make the meaning of the commonest phrase appear absolutely 14_____. He was a 15_____, from his youth up employed in these parts—nothing more. He was obeyed, yet he inspired neither love nor fear, nor even respect. He inspired uneasiness. That was it! Uneasiness.

Jane Austen: Original Gangsta

One thing's for sure about nineteenth century England: At that time, the country was all about guns, bitches, and bling*. So it only makes sense to read Jane Austen's *Pride and Prejudice* in its intended vernacular, even if that style was not presently invented. This style is, of course, ghetto-fabulous street speak. It's the only language a baller like Mr. Collins could use to propose to a fine-ass woman like Elizabeth. Fill in the blanks to read Elizabeth's response. Be sure to replace that old English stuffiness with some crunk-tastic Old English 800.

HINT: You may want to read the passage (instead of choosing words blindly) to decide which urban phrases will fit best.

SYNONYM FOR "REALLY" (AS IN "YOU LISTEN HERE NOW." EXAMPLES: A'IGHT. WORD. FO SHO)	1	_____
"YOU PUZZLE ME EXCEEDINGLY" (REPLACE "PUZZLE ME EXCEEDINGLY." EXAMPLES: YOU ARE LOCO. CRUNK. TRIPPIN')	2	_____
SYNONYM FOR "ENCOURAGEMENT"	3	_____
SYNONYM FOR "TRUE" (EXAMPLES: FO REAL. FO SHIZZLE)	4	_____
"YOU MUST ALLOW ME TO FLATTER MYSELF" (REPLACE THE WORD "FLATTER" IN THIS PHRASE)	5	_____
ADJECTIVE	6	_____
NOUN	7	_____
SYNONYM FOR "HIGHLY DESIRABLE"	8	_____
SYNONYM FOR "MONEY" (EXAMPLES: DUCKETS. CHEDDAR. BENJAMINS)	9	_____
NAME OF A GANG	10	_____
SYNONYM FOR YOUR "FAMILY" (OR YOUR "PEOPLE")	11	_____
LARGE SEXUALIZED FEMALE BODY PART	12	_____
SYNONYM FOR "REJECTION"	13	_____
SYNONYM FOR "WOMEN"	14	_____

*BY GUNS, BITCHES, AND BLING, WE MEAN IMPERIALISM, THE QUEEN, AND THE CROWN JEWELS.

"1_____, Mr. Collins," cried Elizabeth, with some warmth, "you 2_____. If what I have hitherto said can appear to you in the form of 3_____, I know not how to express my refusal in such a way as may convince you of its being 4_____."

"You must give me leave to 5_____myself, my dear cousin, that your refusal of my addresses are merely words of course . . . It does not appear to me that my hand is 6_____, or that the 7_____ I can offer would be any other than 8_____. My 9_____, my connections with 10_____, and my relationship to your 11_____, are the circumstances highly in my favor; and you should take it into further consideration that, in spite of your 12_____ it is by no means certain that another offer of marriage may ever be made to you. . . . As I must, therefore, conclude that you are not serious in your 13_____. I shall choose to attribute it to your wish of increasing my love by suspense, according to the usual practice of all 14_____."

E! True Hollywood (JUST SO) Stories

Rudyard Kipling helps explain how all the animals came to be the way they are in his *Just So Stories*. Now, when you go to the zoo, you know for certain that an elephant has a long nose because a crocodile pulled it. It's science. If only Kipling had helped us by describing the animals of another zoo: Hollywood. For instance, how did Sarah Jessica Parker's nose get that way? Oh, the paparazzi pulled it? Makes sense.

FILL IN THE BLANKS TO HEAR SOME MORE E! TRUE HOLLYWOOD (JUST SO) STORIES.

AN OCCUPATION IN HOLLYWOOD	1	_____
OCCUPATION FROM #1	2	_____
OCCUPATION FROM #1	3	_____
A FAMOUS ACTRESS	4	_____
PROMINENT PHYSICAL FEATURE ON ACTRESS FROM #4 (PLURAL)	5	_____
ACTRESS FROM #4	6	_____
ANOTHER PROMINENT BODY PART ON ACTRESS FROM #4	7	_____
A FAMOUS ACTOR	8	_____
PROMINENT BODY PART ON ACTOR FROM #8	9	_____
ADJECTIVE TO DESCRIBE #8	10	_____
ACTOR FROM #8	11	_____
BODY PART FROM #9	12	_____
PLUS-SIZED ACTRESS	13	_____
PROMINENT BODY PARTS ON ACTRESS FROM #13 (PLURAL)	14	_____
ADJECTIVE TO DESCRIBE #14	15	_____
ACTRESS FROM #13	16	_____
BODY PART	17	_____
ADJECTIVE TO DESCRIBE A PARTY ANIMAL	18	_____
ACTOR WHO HAS HAD WILD TIMES	19	_____
A TYPE OF DRUG OR ALCOHOL	20	_____
ADJECTIVE FROM #18	21	_____
ACTOR FROM #19	22	_____
ADJECTIVE TO DESCRIBE A FALL-DOWN DRUNK	23	_____
ADJECTIVE TO DESCRIBE A GYM RAT	24	_____
DIRTY BODY PART	25	_____

The was one 1_____—a new 2_____—a
3_____'s child—who was full of 'satiable curiosity, and
that means he asked ever so many questions. . . . He asked his tall aunt,
4_____, why her 5_____ grew just
so, and his tall aunt 6_____ spanked him with her hard, hard
7_____. He asked his tall uncle, 8_____, what
made his 9_____ 10_____, and his tall
uncle, 11_____, spanked him with his hard, hard
12_____. And still he was full of 'satiable curiosity! He asked his
broad aunt, 13_____, why her 14_____ were
15_____, and his broad aunt, 16_____,
spanked him with her broad, broad 17_____; and he asked his
18_____ uncle, 19_____, why 20_____
tasted just so, and his 21_____ uncle, 22_____,
spanked him with his 23_____, 24_____
25_____. And still he was full of 'satiable curiosity.

Moby _____ Tease

One message from *Moby Dick*—the tale of a sea captain who obsessively pursues a large, vindictive whale—is that it is necessary to have goals in life, but striving after them monomaniacally will lead to self-destruction and harm to others. How would this story unfold if Ishmael (the novel's narrator) were replaced by another figure? Perhaps a stripper? (For one, the book would probably include a lot less mundane detail about the whaling industry.) Having worked all night surrounded by "sperm whales" of a different sort, this working girl knows exactly when to count her change and call it quits.

FILL IN THE BLANKS BELOW TO FIND OUT HOW SHE LETS OFF STEAM AND PREVENTS HERSELF FROM HARPOONING SOME BLUBBERY JERK WITH A STILETTO.

STRIPPER NAME	1	_____
A DURATION OF TIME (PLURAL)	2	_____
ITEM OF WOMEN'S CLOTHING	3	_____
A STREET NAME (INCLUDE STREET, AVENUE, BOULEVARD, ETC. AT THE END)	4	_____
VERB	5	_____
ADJECTIVE	6	_____
ADJECTIVE	7	_____
BODY PART	8	_____
ADJECTIVE (TO DESCRIBE A RABID DOG)	9	_____
ADJECTIVE (TO DESCRIBE A LANDFILL)	10	_____
MAJOR RETAIL CHAIN OR FAST FOOD JOINT	11	_____
TYPE OF SOCIAL GATHERING, MEETING, OR CELEBRATION	12	_____
A MENTAL DISORDER	13	_____
HANDYMAN'S TOOL OR POWER TOOL	14	_____
BODY PART (PLURAL)	15	_____
A RELAXING PLACE (ESPECIALLY FOR A STRIPPER)	16	_____

Call me 1_____. Some 2_____ ago—never mind how long precisely—having little or no money in my 3_____, and nothing particular to interest me on 4_____, I thought I would 5_____ about a little and see the 6_____ part of the world. It is a way I have of driving off the spleen, and regulating the circulation. Whenever I find myself growing 7_____ about the 8_____; whenever it is a 9_____, 10_____ November in my soul; whenever I find myself involuntarily pausing before 11_____, and bringing up the rear of every 12_____ I meet; and especially whenever my 13_____ gets such an upper hand of me, that it requires a strong 14_____ to prevent me from deliberately stepping into the street, and methodically knocking people's 15_____ off—then, I account it high time to get to 16_____ as soon as I can.

Neverland Office Park

We always think of Neverland as the place where kids never grow up. But let's face it, some kids want nothing more than to grow up. Some kids like being the banker more than they like actually playing Monopoly. Some kids, when they play doctor, make you fill out insurance paperwork. And *Peter Pan* would be a very different book with these kids. So come! Follow me to a land of magic! Full of spreadsheets and punch clocks! Where the only Captain Hook you'll find is a guy in a strip mall selling "towel hanging solutions." Go to the first cubicle on the left and straight on till morning...

EXCITING PROFESSION	1	_____
EXCITING PROFESSION FROM #1	2	_____
BORING PROFESSION	3	_____
BORING CITY	4	_____
NOUN RELATED TO THE BORING PROFESSION (PLURAL)	5	_____
ADJECTIVE	6	_____
BORING PROFESSION FROM #3 (PLURAL)	7	_____
BORING PROFESSION FROM #3 (PLURAL)	8	_____
ADJECTIVE	9	_____
NEGATIVE ADJECTIVE	10	_____
DIRTY VERB ENDING IN –ING	11	_____
BORING PROFESSION FROM #3 (PLURAL)	12	_____
PROFESSION RELATED TO PROFESSION IN #3	13	_____
VERB RELATED TO PROFESSION IN #13 (PAST TENSE)	14	_____
NOUN RELATED TO PROFESSION IN #13	15	_____
BORING PROFESSION FROM #3 (PLURAL)	16	_____

"It was because I heard father and mother," he explained in a low voice, "talking about what I was to be when I became a 1_____."

He was extraordinarily agitated now. "I don't want ever to be a

2_____," he said with passion. "I want always to

be a 3_____ and to have fun. So I ran away to

4_____ and lived a long long time among the

5_____."

She gave him a look of the most 6_____ admiration, and he thought it was because he had run away, but it was really because he knew 7_____. Wendy had lived such a home life that to know

8_____ struck her as quite 9_____.

She poured out questions about them, to his surprise, for they were

rather 10_____ to him, getting in his way and so on,

and indeed he sometimes had to give them a 11_____.

Still, he liked them on the whole, and he told her about the beginning of

12_____.

"You see, Wendy, when the first 13_____ 14_____

for the first time, its 15_____ broke into a thousand pieces,

and they all went skipping about, and that was the beginning of

16_____."

Tarzan, King Of the Jungle Gym

Tarzan from Edgar Rice Burroughs's *Tarzan King of the Apes* is always seen as the hunky, dreamy, untamed jungle man of every woman's fantasy. But come on, ladies...When was the last time a man tried to impress you by beating on his chest and yelling? Or by swinging from a vine? Or by eating weird things off the ground? It was probably elementary school. And let's face it, Tarzan's writings to Jane do sound like the kind of love letter you write to a girl right after you punch her and tell her she has cooties. Fill in the blanks to read Tarzan's playground penmanship.

FULL NAME OF YOUR ELEMENTARY SCHOOL (EXAMPLE: JAMES WILEY ELEMENTARY SCHOOL)	1	_____
PIECE OF PLAYGROUND EQUIPMENT	2	_____
SOMETHING CHILDREN PLAY WITH (PLURAL)	3	_____
TYPE OF FOOD FOUND IN A KID'S LUNCH (PLURAL)	4	_____
A TOY FOUND ON A PLAYGROUND (PLURAL)	5	_____
AN OUTDOOR PLACE WHERE CHILDREN PLAY	6	_____
VERB (SOMETHING CHILDREN DO TO SHOW OFF)	7	_____
NAME OF YOUR ELEMENTARY SCHOOL	8	_____
NOUN FORM OF VERB IN # 7 (PLURAL) (EXAMPLE: HUNT/HUNTER, JUMP/JUMPER, ETC.)	9	_____
VERB (SOMETHING ELSE KIDS DO TO SHOW OFF)	10	_____
NAME OF YOUR ELEMENTARY SCHOOL	11	_____
NOUN FORM OF VERB IN #10 (PLURAL)	12	_____
SOMETHING CHILDREN USE TO CARRY THEIR THINGS	13	_____
FULL NAME OF YOUR ELEMENTARY SCHOOL	14	_____
YOUR STRICTEST TEACHER	15	_____
TYPE OF KID AT SCHOOL (EXAMPLE: BULLY, NERD, PASTE-EATER, ETC.)	16	_____
ANOTHER PIECE OF PLAYGROUND EQUIPMENT	17	_____
PLACE FROM #6	18	_____
ANOTHER PIECE OF PLAYGROUND EQUIPMENT	19	_____
FULL NAME OF YOUR ELEMENTARY SCHOOL	20	_____

While he waited he passed the time printing a message to her; whether he intended giving it to her he himself could not have told, but he took infinite pleasure in seeing his thoughts expressed in print—in which he was not so uncivilized after all. He wrote:

I am Tarzan of 1_____. I want you. I am yours.
You are mine. We will live here together always in my
2_____. I will bring you the best 3_____,
and the tenderest 4_____, the finest 5_____
that roam the 6_____. I will 7_____
for you. I am the greatest of the 8_____
9_____. I will 10_____ for you. I am
the mightiest of the 11_____ 12_____.
You are Jane Porter, I saw it in your 13_____.
When you see this you will know that it is for you and that
Tarzan of 14_____ loves you.

As he stood, straight as 15_____, by the door, waiting after he had finished the message, there came to his keen ears a familiar sound. It was the passing of a 16_____ through the 17_____ of the 18_____.

For an instant he listened intently, and then from the 19_____ came the agonized scream of a woman, and Tarzan of 20_____, dropping his first love letter upon the ground, shot like a panther into the forest.

Bad Little Women

Ahhhh, *Little Women*. A classic book about what it means to be a young lady. A novel about what it means to grow up... on the wrong side of the tracks. You heard me. What sort of lightweight pushover do you take Louisa May Alcott for? Meg, Jo, Beth, and Amy grew up on the streets. The streets of *Concord, Massachusetts*. It's real out there, man. These aren't just little women, these are *bad* little women.

CAR THAT MIGHT BELONG TO A RAPPER	1	_____
DANGEROUS OR SEXY ADJECTIVE	2	_____
TYPE OF WOMEN'S UNDERGARMENT (PLURAL)	3	_____
TRADITIONALLY MALE OCCUPATION (PLURAL)	4	_____
A FIERCE BREED OF DOG (PLURAL)	5	_____
GANGSTA TERM FOR "MONEY"	6	_____
TYPE OF ALCOHOL (PLURAL)	7	_____
SYNONYM FOR "CLEARHEADED"	8	_____
NAME FOR A TYPE OF DANCE (THE MACARENA, THE ELECTRIC SLIDE, ETC.)	9	_____
AN ILLICIT PROFESSION	10	_____
TYPE OF PRESCRIPTION DRUG	11	_____
SLANG FOR "CAR"	12	_____
SYNONYM FOR "SIN"	13	_____
A MID-SIZED AMERICAN CITY	14	_____
BORING ITEM (PLURAL)	15	_____
BORING ITEM (PLURAL)	16	_____
BORING ITEM (PLURAL)	17	_____
SYNONYM FOR "SERVANT" (PLURAL)	18	_____
ITEM FOUND AT A STRIP CLUB (PLURAL)	19	_____
STREET SLANG FOR "COOL"	20	_____
FAMOUS, POSSIBLY VIOLENT, HIP-HOP STAR	21	_____
TYPE OF ILLEGAL DRUG	22	_____
ANOTHER ILLEGAL DRUG	23	_____
A VERY DANGEROUS PET	24	_____

Margaret seemed to find it a little hard to tell hers, and waved a brake before her face, as if to disperse imaginary gnats while she said slowly, "I should like a lovely 1_____, full of all sorts of 2_____ things—nice food, pretty 3_____, handsome 4_____, pleasant 5_____, and heaps of 6_____. I am to be mistress of it, and manage it as I like, with plenty of 7_____, so I never need to work 8_____. How I should enjoy it! For I wouldn't be idle, but do 9_____, and make everyone love me dearly."

. . . "Why don't you say you'd have a splendid, wise, good 10_____ and some 11_____? You know your 12_____ wouldn't be perfect without," said blunt Jo, who had no tender fancies yet, and rather scorned 13_____, except in 14_____.

"You'd have nothing but 15_____, 16_____, and 17_____ in yours," answered Meg petulantly.

"Wouldn't I though? I have a stable full of Arabian 18_____, rooms piled high with 19_____, and I'd write out of a 20_____ inkstand, so that my works should be as famous as 21_____."

"Mine is to stay at home safe with 22_____ and 23_____, and help take care of the 24_____," said Beth contentedly.

Roxanne, you don't have to turn on the red badge of courage

You've heard it before...war is hell. Stephen Crane explored that in *The Red Badge of Courage*. His main character, Henry Fleming, would gladly go back to boring chores on the farm than fight in the Civil War. You've heard this before, too...love is hell. Crane didn't explore that, so we will! Watch what happens to Henry when he leaves his boring job to become an...um...gentleman of the night. Depending on the time of month, the red badge of courage could take on a whole new meaning for Henry.

PIZZA DELIVERY PLACE	1	_____
DELIVERY PLACE FROM #1	2	_____
EVENT WHERE YOU WOULD FIND PIZZA	3	_____
DELIVERY PLACE FROM #1	4	_____
ANOTHER EVENT WHERE YOU WOULD FIND PIZZA	5	_____
DELIVERY PLACE FROM #1	6	_____
ANOTHER EVENT WHERE YOU WOULD FIND PIZZA	7	_____
DELIVERY PLACE FROM #1	8	_____
NAME OF A FRATERNITY	9	_____
NAME OF YOUR FIRST BOSS	10	_____
NAME OF YOUR ANNOYING COWORKER	11	_____
ITEM FOUND IN A PIZZA PLACE (PLURAL)	12	_____
SEX TOY (PLURAL)	13	_____
A STREET WHERE SKETCHY THINGS HAPPEN	14	_____
SYNONYM FOR "PROSTITUTE"	15	_____
SEXUAL VERB	16	_____
FEMALE-DOMINATED OCCUPATION (PLURAL)	17	_____
SKETCHY LOCATION IN YOUR CITY	18	_____

He wished, without reserve, that he was at 1_____

again making the endless rounds from the 2_____ to

the 3_____, from the 4_____ to

the 5_____, from the 6_____ to the

7_____, from the 8_____ to the

9_____ house. He remembered he had often cursed

10_____ and 11_____, and had sometimes

flung 12_____. But, from his present point of view, there

was a halo of happiness about each of their heads, and he would have

sacrificed all the 13_____ on 14_____ to

have been enabled to return to them. He told himself that he was not

formed for a 15_____. And he mused seriously upon the

radical differences between himself and the men who were

16_____ing 17_____ around 18_____.

Aesop's XXX Fables

Sure, language is a fluid thing, always changing, always evolving. So it's understandable that the meaning of words may change through the ages. But come on, surely Aesop knew better than to name one of his fables *The Ass and His Masters*, right? That's like naming your city Bangkok or your racecar driver Dick Trickle; you're gonna get some snickers. So please, give in fully to the immature middle-school kid inside you, and fill in the blanks to enjoy this updated fable: *Assmasters*.

A CELEBRITY WITH A BIG BEHIND	1	_____
FURNITURE TO SIT ON (PLURAL)	2	_____
NAME OF A PLASTIC SURGEON (REAL OR MADE-UP)	3	_____
SURGEON FROM #3	4	_____
SYNONYM FOR "ATTACHED"	5	_____
A CELEBRITY WITH A REGULAR-SIZED BEHIND	6	_____
ADJECTIVE (ENDING IN –ER)	7	_____
AN UNCOMFORTABLE PIECE OF FURNITURE TO SIT ON (PLURAL)	8	_____
NAME OF A GYM	9	_____
ANOTHER PHRASE FOR THE LOWER BODY	10	_____
SYNONYM FOR "ATTACHED"	11	_____
A CELEBRITY WITH A VERY SMALL BEHIND	12	_____
NAME FROM #12	13	_____
SOUND A BUTT MAKES (ENDING IN –ING)	14	_____
SYNONYM FOR "USED"	15	_____

AN ASS, belonging to 1_____ who gave him too little 2_____ and too much work made a petition to 3_____ to be released from his present service and provided with another master. 4_____, after warning him that he would repent his request, caused him to be 5_____ to 6_____. Shortly afterwards, finding that he had 7_____ 8_____ and harder work in the 9_____, he petitioned for another change of master. 10_____, telling him that it would be the last time that he could grant his request, ordained that he be 11_____ to 12_____. The Ass found that he had fallen into worse hands, and noting 13_____'s occupation, said, 14_____: "It would have been better for me to have been either starved by the one, or to have been overworked by the other of my former masters, than to have been 15_____ by my present owner . . ."

I Love You, Man (Friday)

In *Robinson Crusoe*, our main character saves the life of Man Friday, a native to the island, teaches him English, and converts him to Christianity. Now, this is a fine thing to teach someone in 1719. After all, they have to spend Sundays together doing something, right? But a modern man would probably teach Man Friday about a much more popular Sunday ritual: ESPN. Fill in the blanks to see what happens when Crusoe and Friday totally bro out over some sports.

A MAJOR LEAGUE SPORT 1 _____

SYNONYM FOR "PLAYED" (AS IN "A GAME WAS PLAYED.") 2 _____

NICKNAME RELATED TO THE SPORT IN #1 3 _____

A BRAND OF BEER 4 _____

A GAME-DAY SNACK FOOD 5 _____

ANOTHER BRAND OF BEER, PERHAPS CHEAPER 6 _____

ANOTHER SNACK FOOD 7 _____

A TEAM FROM THIS SPORT 8 _____

A FAMOUS PLAYER ON THE TEAM FROM #8 9 _____

AN ACTION IN THIS SPORT (EXAMPLE: SHOOTING BASKETS, SCORING GOALS, HIGH STICKING, ETC.) 10 _____

SOMEONE WHO WORKS IN SPORTS (NOT AN ATHLETE) 11 _____

SOMEONE ELSE WHO WORKS IN SPORTS 12 _____

A UNIT OF TIME IN THIS SPORT (EXAMPLE: HALF TIME, NINTH INNING, ETC.) 13 _____

ANOTHER FAMOUS PLAYER IN THIS SPORT 14 _____

AN AREA IN A STADIUM THAT IS HARD TO SEE FROM 15 _____

I let him know that his name was to be Friday, which was the day on which 1_____ was 2_____, and I taught him that he was to call me 3_____.

Taking a cup of 4_____, I drank some of it and moistened my 5_____ in some. I gave Friday a cup of 6_____; he did the same thing with his 7_____, showing by signs that he thought it very good . . .

Friday, after a while, knew 8_____ so well that I could talk to him about anything that I wished.

I taught him that there is 9_____ who made everything and that He loves 10_____ as a father loves his children, and that He cares for 11_____ even more tenderly than does a 12_____. When 13_____ came I taught him about 14_____.

I told him how I happened to be on the 15_____, and how long I had been there and what a hard time I had had at first to get food and make a home, and how lonely I had been until he came.

A Poem Not So Revered

Henry Wadsworth Longfellow's "The Midnight Ride of Paul Revere" is a staple of American literature. Not to be outdone, Henry's lesser known younger brother, Dickie Filburt Longfellow, tried to write a poem of his own. It was about the lesser known brother of Paul Revere, who, also not to be outdone by his brother, went on a long horsey ride, too. Both Dickie's poem and the ride of the lesser known Revere brother are obscure (and for good reason). However, due to a need for more pages in this book, we have decided to reprint it. So please, enjoy the worst that sibling rivalry has to offer...

OCCUPATION (PLURAL)	1	_____
TIME OF DAY	2	_____
A SILLY FIRST NAME	3	_____
A HIGH ORDINAL NUMBER, (EXAMPLE: 27TH, 33RD, 41ST, 102ND)	4	_____
A CREATURE	5	_____
SCI-FI OR FANTASY CREATURE FROM BOOKS, TV, OR MOVIES (PLURAL) (EXAMPLE: HOBBITS, EWOKS, SMURFS, ETC.)	6	_____
TYPE OF UNDERGARMENT	7	_____
STORE IN THE MALL	8	_____
ADJECTIVE	9	_____
ADJECTIVE	10	_____
TITLE OF AN ADULT MAGAZINE (PLURAL)	11	_____
ADJECTIVE	12	_____
CHARACTERS FROM #6 (PLURAL)	13	_____
OCCUPATION (PLURAL)	14	_____
A STORE YOU HATE TO VISIT	15	_____
CHARACTERS FROM #6	16	_____
A SEXUAL VERB	17	_____

Listen, my 1_____, and you shall hear

Of the 2_____ ride of 3_____ Revere,

On the 4_____ of April, in Seventy-five:

Hardly a 5_____ is now alive

Who remembers that famous day and year.

He said to his friend, "If the 6_____ march

By land or sea from the town to-night,

Hang a 7_____ aloft in the belfry arch

Of the 8_____ as a signal-light,

One, if by land, and two, if by sea;

And I on the 9_____ shore will be,

Ready to ride and spread the alarm

Through every 10_____ village and farm,

For the country folk to be up and to arm."

You know the rest. In the 11_____ you have read,

How the 12_____ 13_____ fired and fled,

How the 14_____ gave them ball for ball,

From behind each fence and 15_____ wall,

Chasing the 16_____ down the lane,

Then crossing the fields to emerge again

Under the trees at the turn of the road,

And only pausing to 17_____ and load.

Pass the bong my dear Watson

Sure, sure, sure, Sherlock Holmes was a masterful detective who could solve cases that no one else could. Sure, sure, he was so awesome that one time he even figured out that the murderer was actually an orang-utan. Sure, he liked to be the smartest guy in the room. But you know what else he liked to do? He liked to get *hiiiiiiiigh*. Let's celebrate the opium addict in our dear Sherlock by reading this passage from *A Study in Scarlet* not as if it was written by Sir Arthur Conan Doyle, but as if it was written by Trance, that guy from college who always wanted you to play Ultimate Frisbee with him.

TITLE OF A BOOK ADVOCATING DRUG USE (EXAMPLE: *HIGH TIMES*)	1	_____
TYPE OF DRUG	2	_____
TYPE OF DRUG PARAPHERNALIA (EXAMPLE: BONG, PIPE, HOOKAH, ETC.)	3	_____
TYPE OF PERSON WHO SMOKES WEED A LOT	4	_____
A MAGICAL PLACE	5	_____
A MUCH MORE LAME PLACE	6	_____
TRIPPY DRUG	7	_____
GROOVY DRUG	8	_____
SOMETHING IN A HIPPIE'S APARTMENT	9	_____
SOMETHING ELSE IN A HIPPIE'S APARTMENT	10	_____
SOMETHING ELSE IN A HIPPIE'S APARTMENT	11	_____
HIPPIE ARTICLE OF CLOTHING	12	_____
HIPPIE ACCESSORY	13	_____
SYNONYM FOR "GROOVYNESS" (SUGGESTED ENDING IN "-NESS" OR ADDING "FACTOR." EXAMPLE: MELLOWNESS, CHILL-FACTOR)	14	_____

Its somewhat ambitious title was 1_____, and it attempted to show how much an observant man might learn by an accurate and systematic examination of 2_____ that came in his way. It struck me as being a remarkable mixture of shrewdness and of absurdity. The reasoning was close and intense, but the deductions appeared to me to be far-fetched and exaggerated. . . .

"From a 3_____ of water," said the writer, "a 4_____ could infer the possibility of 5_____ or a 6_____ without having seen or heard of one or the other. So all life is a great chain, the nature of which is known whenever we are shown a single link of it. Like all other arts, the Science of 7_____ and 8_____ is one which can only be acquired by a long and patient study. . . . By a man's 9_____, by his 10_____, by his 11_____, by his 12_____, by the callosities of his forefinger and thumb, by his expression, by his 13_____—by each of these things a man's 14_____ is plainly revealed. That all united should fail to enlighten the competent enquirer in any case is almost inconceivable."

 Vanity Fair (no. not the one by Conde Nast)

Vanity Fair? You mean like the magazine? Yeah, the one that lists what kind of trouble the hot young celebrities are getting into in Los Angeles. Oh, you mean the book? *Vanity Fair* by William Makepeace Thackeray ... OK ... what's it about? It's about a young woman who tries to climb the socialite ladder and seduces men to control them for her own personal benefit? Oh, OK ... so you *do* mean the magazine about hot young celebrities?

NAME OF A CLOTHING DESIGNER	1	_____
BRAND OF DIGITAL CAMERA (PLURAL)	2	_____
NEGATIVE ADJECTIVE	3	_____
ADJECTIVE TO DESCRIBE SOMEONE WHO'S HAD TOO MANY	4	_____
A-LIST CELEBRITY	5	_____
SUPER HOT NIGHT CLUB	6	_____
A TYPE OF MAN AT A HIP PARTY (PLURAL)	7	_____
A NEIGHBORHOOD IN LOS ANGELES	8	_____
B-LIST CELEBRITY LAST NAME	9	_____
VERB	10	_____
NOUN (PLURAL)	11	_____
HOLLYWOOD OCCUPATION (PLURAL)	12	_____
VERB (RELATED TO DRUG USE)	13	_____
ADJECTIVE	14	_____

Mrs. Rawdon Crawley's début was, on the contrary, very brilliant. She arrived very late. Her face was radiant; her dress 1_____.
In the midst of the great persons assembled, and the 2_____ directed to her, Rebecca seemed to be as 3_____ and 4_____ as when she used to marshal 5_____'s little girls to 6_____. Numbers of the men she knew already, and the 7_____ thronged round her. As for the ladies, it was whispered among them that Rawdon had run away with her from out of 8_____, and that she was a relation of the 9_____ family. She 10_____ 11_____ so perfectly that there might be some truth in this report, and it was agreed that her manners were fine, and her air *distingué*. Fifty would-be 12_____ thronged round her at once, and pressed to have the honor to 13_____ with her. . . . She vowed that it was a 14_____ ball; that there was everybody that every one knew, and only a very few nobodies in the whole room.

If I Only Had A C@#k

When Dorothy first meets the Wizard in *The Wonderful Wizard of Oz*, he's not very nice. In fact he's kind of a jerk. In fact, if we weren't in mixed company right now, there's a certain dirty body part I'd use to describe him. It's like Dorothy expected this majestic and wise man and instead she gets...you know. It makes a girl wonder: "I followed the yellow brick road for *this*?"

FILL IN THE BLANKS TO SEE HOW SHE REACTS.

COLOR	1	_____
UNUSUAL BUILDING MATERIAL	2	_____
NOUN	3	_____
NOUN (PLURAL)	4	_____
PRIVATE BODY PART	5	_____
BODY PART FROM #5	6	_____
BODY PART FROM #5	7	_____
ANIMAL	8	_____
ADVERB	9	_____
ADVERB	10	_____
SPECIFIC PART OF THE BODY PART FROM #5	11	_____
ADJECTIVE	12	_____
ADJECTIVE	13	_____
BODY PART FROM #5	14	_____
ADJECTIVE	15	_____

But what interested Dorothy most was the big throne of 1_____

2_____ that stood in the middle of the room. It was

shaped like a 3_____ and sparkled with

4_____, as did everything else. In the center of the chair

was an enormous 5_____, without a body to

support it or any arms or legs whatever. There was no hair upon his

6_____, but it had eyes and a nose and a mouth, and

was much bigger than the 7_____ of the biggest

8_____.

　　As Dorothy gazed upon this in wonder and fear, the eyes turned

slowly and looked at her 9_____ and 10_____.

Then the 11_____ moved, and Dorothy heard a voice say:

　　"I am Oz, the Great and 12_____. Who are you and why

do you seek me?"

　　It was not such a(n) 13_____ voice as she expected

to come from the big 14_____; so she took courage

and answered:

　　"I am Dorothy, the Small and 15_____. I have come to you

for help."

willy's big day at the zoo

Want to hear a fun fact?* William Blake wrote his poem "The Tiger" while visiting the London Zoo. And he didn't just write one for the tiger. He wrote one for every animal at the zoo that day. Why haven't you heard of the other poems? Well, there's one right here, but don't judge ol' Willy B. too much, OK? I mean, he wasn't at his usual writing desk. He was at the zoo.**

A GOOFY LOOKING ANIMAL	1	_____
ANIMAL FROM #1	2	_____
A STORE IN THE MALL	3	_____
ADJECTIVE	4	_____
BODY PART	5	_____
ADJECTIVE	6	_____
A NON-GEOGRAPHIC LOCATION	7	_____
SOMETHING YOU RIDE	8	_____
OCCUPATION	9	_____
AN AVERAGE U.S. CITY	10	_____
ANOTHER GOOFY ANIMAL	11	_____
ANIMAL FROM #1	12	_____
ANIMAL FROM #1	13	_____
ANOTHER STORE IN THE MALL	14	_____
ADJECTIVE	15	_____
VERB	16	_____

* FACT NOT ACTUALLY TRUE.

** HE WAS NOT AT THE ZOO. IN FACT HE DIDN'T WRITE THIS. YOU DID. COME ON, YOU KNOW THAT.

1_____, 2_____, burning bright

In the 3_____ of the night,

What 4_____ 5_____ or eye

Could frame thy 6_____ symmetry?

In what distant 7_____ or skies

Burnt the fire of thine eyes?

On what 8_____ dare he aspire?

What the hand dare seize the fire?

When the 9_____ threw down their spears,

And water'd 10_____ with their tears,

Did He smile His work to see?

Did He who made the 11_____ make thee?

12_____, 13_____, burning bright

In the 14_____ of the night,

What 15_____ hand or eye

Dare 16_____ thy fearful symmetry?

Dorian Gray, Purveyor of Bad Art

The problem with the protagonist in Oscar Wilde's *The Picture of Dorian Gray* is not that he bargained his soul for immortality, it's that he picked the wrong type of art. Do you really want to watch a picture of yourself decay for all eternity? How mortifying. No, go to the flea market and pick something that's already bad. Entrust your soul with *Dogs Playing Poker*. Or maybe invest your immortality in *Elvis on Velvet*. What's the worst that happens? The decay can't make the art worse. Fill in the blanks to see what kind of bad art Dorian chooses.

POPULAR ICON (MALE OR FEMALE, FREQUENTLY THE SUBJECT OF TACKY ART)	1	_____
ADJECTIVE	2	_____
ADJECTIVE	3	_____
ADJECTIVE	4	_____
NAME FROM #1	5	_____
COLOR	6	_____
NAME FROM #1	7	_____
NAME FROM #1	8	_____
COLOR	9	_____
COLOR	10	_____
ANOTHER OBJECT IN THE PAINTING, SOMETHING THE ICON WOULD HOLD/CARRY/KEEP	11	_____
OBJECT IN A YARD SALE	12	_____
SYNONYM FOR "BOUGHT"	13	_____
NAME FROM #1	14	_____
EXPRESSION SIMILAR TO "CREAM OF THE CROP"	15	_____
NAME OF A FRIEND OR FAMILY MEMBER	16	_____
ODD LOCATION FOR A MEETING	17	_____

Yet 1_____ was watching him, with [his/her]

2_____ face and [his/her] 3_____ smile.

[His/Her] 4_____ hair gleamed in the early sunlight.

5_____'s 6_____ eyes met his own. A sense of

infinite pity, not for 7_____, but for the painted image of

8_____, came over him. It had altered already, and would

alter more. Its 9_____ would wither into 10_____.

Its 11_____ would die. For every 12_____ that

he 13_____, a stain would fleck and wreck

14_____. But he would not sin. The picture, changed

or unchanged, would be to him the 15_____. He would resist

temptation. He would not see 16_____ any more—would

not, at any rate, listen to those subtle poisonous theories that in Basil

Hallward's 17_____ had first stirred within him the

passion for impossible things.

Ugh. Bridge and Tunnel People are So... undead

Visiting a big city for the first time can be an intimidating experience. There's an enormous culture shock when you go from hometown meat and potatoes to uptown macrobiotics and pedicures. It's very similar to how the monster felt in Mary Shelley's *Frankenstein* when he saw other humans for the first time. So let this be a lesson to you, urbanites: When someone from Smallsville, U.S.A., comes to visit, be sure to be nice, give them directions, and recommend good neighborhood restaurants. If you're not nice, they may turn out to be the reanimated undead capable of smashing in your skull.

A LUXURY ITEM (PLURAL)	1	_____
ANOTHER LUXURY ITEM (PLURAL)	2	_____
LOW-STATUS OCCUPATION	3	_____
SLANG FOR "LOSER"	4	_____
SYNONYM FOR "SELL"	5	_____
GOOD OR SERVICE SOLD BY #3 (PLURAL)	6	_____
HIGH-STATUS OCCUPATION (PLURAL)	7	_____
SOMETHING CITY DWELLERS LIKE (PLURAL)	8	_____
SOMETHING ELSE CITY DWELLERS LIKE (PLURAL)	9	_____
SOMETHING ELSE CITY DWELLERS LIKE (PLURAL)	10	_____
SOMETHING ELSE CITY DWELLERS LIKE (PLURAL)	11	_____
SOMETHING ELSE CITY DWELLERS LIKE (PLURAL)	12	_____
ADJECTIVE DESCRIBING SOMETHING RURAL	13	_____
ADJECTIVE DESCRIBING SOMETHING ELSE RURAL	14	_____
A FAMOUS CITY DWELLER	15	_____
FOOD YOU WOULD GET FROM A COUNTRY ROADSTOP	16	_____
NAME OF A BIG CITY	17	_____

The words induced me to turn towards myself. I learned that the possession most esteemed by your fellow-creatures were

1_____ and 2_____ united with riches. A man might be respected with only one of these acquisitions; but without either he was considered, except in very rare instances, as a

3_____ and a 4_____, doomed to

5_____ his 6_____ for the profit of the

7_____. And what was I? Of 8_____ and

9_____ I was absolutely ignorant; but I knew that I possessed no 10_____, no 11_____, no kind of 12_____. I was, besides, endowed with a figure hideously 13_____ and 14_____;

I was not even of the same nature as 15_____. I was more agile than they, and could subsist upon 16_____;

I bore the extremes of heat and cold with less injury to my frame; my stature far exceeded theirs. When I looked around, I saw and heard of none like me. Was I then a monster, a blot upon

17_____, from which all men fled, and whom all men disowned?

Do Brown Pennies Spend at Strip Clubs?

(PHONE RINGS.)

"Hey, Yeats? It's your editor. Listen, I just read the poem you sent over. The one about the brown penny and love and all that? Yeah, it's uh, it's very sweet. Like, *too* sweet. I mean, I dunno the kinda broads you're getting with, WB, but if I tried to take my ol' ball and chain out on the town with just a penny in my pocket? Man, I'd be riding the couch for months after that. I made some changes. You know, just so the poem reflects the kinda girl you get for just a penny. Let me know what you think."

VERB (PAST TENSE. RELATED TO SPEAKING) (EXAMPLE: SPOKE. WHISPERED. YELLED. ETC.)	1	_____
ADJECTIVE	2	_____
ANTONYM OF WORD IN #2	3	_____
SLANG TERM FOR HAVING SEX	4	_____
UNFLATTERING ADJECTIVE	5	_____
UNFLATTERING ADJECTIVE	6	_____
BODY PART	7	_____
ADJECTIVE	8	_____
ADJECTIVE	9	_____
ANOTHER SLANG TERM FOR HAVING SEX	10	_____
SLANG FOR AN ATTRACTIVE WOMAN (PLURAL)	11	_____
SLANG FOR AN UNATTRACTIVE WOMAN (PLURAL)	12	_____
A GROSS SNACK FOOD	13	_____
SEXUAL VERB	14	_____

I 1_____, 'I am too 2_____,'

And then, 'I am 3_____ enough';

Wherefore I threw a penny

To find out if I might 4_____.

'Go and love, go and love, young man,

If the lady be 5_____ and 6_____.'

Ah, penny, brown penny, brown penny,

I am looped in the loops of her 7_____.

O love is the 8_____ thing,

There is nobody 9_____ enough

To find out all that is in it,

For he would be thinking of 10_____

Till the 11_____ had run away

And the 12_____ eaten the 13_____.

Ah, penny, brown penny, brown penny,

One cannot 14_____ it too soon.

Great Expectations, Poor Execution

There are some men, some Casanovas, whose silver tongues can get them any women they want. Then there are the rest of the guys who sweat through first dates, praying that they avoid saying things like, "you got a purty mouth." For Pip in Charles Dickens's *Great Expectations*, he spends his whole life trying to raise himself to a higher station in life for his love, Estella. And this includes not speaking the verbal equivalent of staring at her boobies and drooling. Fill in the blanks to see the confession of love that Pip is trying desperately *not* to make.

TITLE OF A DIRTY MAGAZINE	1	_____
LOW-STATUS OCCUPATION	2	_____
VERB (PAST TENSE)	3	_____
NAME OF A RIVER OR CREEK	4	_____
NAME OF A SHIP	5	_____
AN UNROMANTIC LOCATION	6	_____
ANOTHER UNROMANTIC LOCATION	7	_____
ANOTHER UNROMANTIC LOCATION	8	_____
ANOTHER UNROMANTIC LOCATION	9	_____
ANOTHER UNROMANTIC LOCATION	10	_____
ANOTHER UNROMANTIC LOCATION	11	_____
ANOTHER UNROMANTIC LOCATION	12	_____
SLANG TERM FOR A WOMAN	13	_____
NAME OF A CITY	14	_____
BODY PART	15	_____
FEMALE BODY PART	16	_____
A PHRASE EQUATING TO "SEXUAL FANTASY"	17	_____
A NONSENSE PHRASE THAT IS PART OF A CAT CALL (EXAMPLE: HUBBA HUBBA)	18	_____
ANOTHER NONSENSE PHRASE THAT IS PART OF A CAT CALL	19	_____

You are part of my existence, part of myself. You have been in every

1_____ I have ever read, since I first came here, the rough

2_____ whose poor heart you 3_____

even then. You have been in every prospect I have ever seen since—on

the 4_____, on the sails of the 5_____, on the

marshes, in the 6_____, in the 7_____,

in the 8_____, in the 9_____, in the

10_____, in the 11_____, in

the 12_____. You have been the embodiment of every

13_____ that my mind has ever become acquainted

with. The stones of which the strongest 14_____ buildings

are made, are not more real, or more impossible to be displaced by your

15_____, than your presence and 16_____

have been to me, there and everywhere, and will be. Estella, to

the last hour of my life, you cannot choose but remain part of my

17_____, part of the little 18_____ in me,

part of the 19_____.

Green with Emma-vy

So your ex is with someone else now. It's cool. Doesn't bother you in the least. So what if she's funny and has a great body? Who cares if she went to an Ivy League school and has a great job? You've moved on. It doesn't matter that she writes a column on how to have better sex. She can't be *that* perfect, right? I mean, everyone's got something. This person probably kicks dogs or something. What? She volunteers at an animal shelter? Oh, give me a friggin' break!

In Jane Austen's *Emma*, Harriet knows exactly how you feel. Fill in the blanks to read an alternate version of Mr. Elton coming back with his hot new sexpot who has it all.

YOUR (FEMALE) FRIEND'S LAST NAME	1	_____
A CITY OR TOWN	2	_____
ADJECTIVE	3	_____
ADJECTIVE	4	_____
ADJECTIVE	5	_____
ADJECTIVE	6	_____
A DISH YOU'D BRING TO A POTLUCK	7	_____
BODY PART	8	_____
SEXUAL VERB (PAST TENSE)	9	_____
ADJECTIVE	10	_____
YOUR (FEMALE) FRIEND'S FIRST NAME	11	_____
NAME FROM #1	12	_____
BODY PART (PLURAL)	13	_____
BODY PART (PLURAL)	14	_____
A HIP TOY/ACCESSORY THAT EVERYONE WANTS	15	_____

Human nature is so well disposed towards those who are in interesting situations that a young person who either marries or dies is sure of being kindly spoken of.

A week had not passed since Miss 1_____'s name was first mentioned in 2_____, before she was, by some means or other, discovered to have every recommendation of person and mind—to be 3_____, 4_____, highly 5_____, and perfectly 6_____; and when Mr. Elton himself arrived to triumph in his happy prospects and circulate the fame of her 7_____, there was very little more for him to do than to tell her Christian name, and say whose 8_____ she principally 9_____. . . .

The 10_____ 11_____ 12_____, in addition to all the usual advantages of perfect 13_____ and 14_____, was in possession of a(n) 15_____—a point of some dignity, as well as some convenience.

Dr. Jekyll & Mr. Efron

It's disturbing how a seemingly normal person can have an evil, wanton, and obsessive other side. Serial killers, terrorists, superfans. You know who I'm talking about: perfectly reasonable adults who scream like teenage girls when Miley Cyrus makes an appearance at the mall, and will make you touch their signed T-shirt while they repeat, "she's such a normal person" for ten minutes. Let's explore the dark side of pop-culture fandom by filling in this passage from *The Strange Case of Dr. Jekyll and Mr. Hyde.*

A STORE THAT SELLS VIDEOS, MUSIC, ETC.	1	_____
NAME OF A STREET	2	_____
NAME OF A COWORKER, FRIEND, OR CLOSE RELATIVE	3	_____
VERB (PAST TENSE, RELATED TO WALKING) (EXAMPLE: SKIPPED, TROTTED, RAN, ETC.)	4	_____
RECORD OF A HOT YOUNG BAND (EXAMPLE: THE KILLERS' RECORD, THE JONAS BROTHERS' RECORD, ETC.)	5	_____
STORE FROM #1	6	_____
RECORDS OF A LESS HOT ARTIST (PLURAL) (EXAMPLE: PAT BENATAR RECORDS, YANNI RECORDS, ETC.)	7	_____
NAME FROM #3	8	_____
RUDE NOISE	9	_____
VERB (PAST TENSE, RELATED TO WALKING)	10	_____
AREA IN THE STORE FROM #1	11	_____
BODY PART	12	_____
NOUN (PLURAL)	13	_____
TITLE OF YOUR BOSS	14	_____
TRINKET YOU MIGHT BUY RELATED TO THE BAND IN #4 (KILLERS FLASHLIGHT, KILLERS WRISTBAND, ETC.)	15	_____
BODY PART	16	_____
TITLE FROM #12	17	_____
A ROCK STAR YOU DON'T LIKE	18	_____

It was this way. I came into the 1_____ from

2_____. It seems 3_____ had

4_____ out to look for this 5_____ or what-

ever it is; for the cabinet door was open, and there he [she] was at the far

end of the 6_____ digging among the 7_____.

8_____ looked up when I came in, gave a kind of

9_____, and 10_____ upstairs into the

11_____. It was but for one minute that I saw him [her],

but the air stood upon my 12_____ like

13_____. Sir, if that was my 14_____,

why had he [she] a 15_____ upon his [her]

16_____? If it was my 17_____, why did

he [she] cry out like 18_____, and run from me?

20,000 Re-Edits Under the Sea

This letter from Jules Verne to his editor was found recently in a private collection in Paris...

DEAR EDITOR,

Yeah, I read your notes. What do you mean the giant squid's not scary? It's totally scary! You think just because you had calamari for lunch that a giant squid's not scary? I had escargot, but that doesn't mean I wouldn't be scared of a giant snail. Okay, maybe that was a bad example. Whatever. If you're so smart, why don't *you* write *20,000 Leagues Under The Sea*? Huh? I dare you.

J-Dog Out,

Jules Verne

FILL IN THE BLANKS TO SEE IF YOU CAN DO BETTER THAN A GIANT SQUID.

ADJECTIVE	1	_____
NON-THREATENING SEA CREATURE	2	_____
UNIT OF LENGTH (PLURAL)	3	_____
NAME FOR A BOAT OR SUBMARINE	4	_____
ADJECTIVE	5	_____
COLOR	6	_____
A NUMBER	7	_____
BODY PART (NOT AN ARM!)	8	_____
A CUTE NICKNAME FOR A SEA MONSTER	9	_____
AN ACTOR WITH CURLY HAIR	10	_____
BODY PART	11	_____
ADJECTIVE	12	_____
TYPE OF BIRD	13	_____
ADJECTIVE TO DESCRIBE BREAKFAST FOODS	14	_____
NOUN (PLURAL)	15	_____
NOUN (PLURAL)	16	_____
ANIMAL FROM #3	17	_____
A STRANGE-LOOKING CELEBRITY	18	_____
A NUMBER	19	_____
A BIGGER NUMBER	20	_____

Before my eyes was a 1_____ monster worthy to figure in the legends of the marvelous. It was an immense 2_____, being eight 3_____ long. It swam crossways in the direction of the 4_____ with great speed, watching us with its enormous 5_____ 6_____ eyes. Its 7_____ arms, or rather feet, fixed to its 8_____, that have given the name of 9_____ to these animals, were twice as long as its body, and were twisted like 10_____'s hair. One could see the 250 air-holes on the inner side of the 11_____. The monster's mouth, a 12_____ beak like a 13_____'s, opened and shut vertically. Its tongue, a 14_____ substance, furnished with several rows of 15_____, came out quivering from this veritable pair of 16_____. What a freak of nature, a bird's beak on a 17_____! Its 18_____-like body formed a fleshy mass that might weigh 19_____ to 20_____ lbs. . . . I overcame the horror that inspired me, and, taking a pencil, began to draw it.

Last of the Desk Jockeys

James Fenimore Cooper's *The Last of the Mohicans* tells an epic tale of war and adventure on the home front during the French and Indian War. But let's face it, there aren't that many wars in upper New York these days. The closest thing to a home front war anymore is when Accounts refuses to reimburse your business meals, or when the HR lady makes you do safety training again. So let's blow it out: Full inter-office warfare! Pick your side, pick your weapon (stapler or hole punch), and go forth to defend your department!

POSITION IN YOUR OFFICE (EXAMPLE: ACCOUNTANT, SALESMAN, DESIGNER, ETC.)	1 _____
CHARACTERISTIC OF PERSON IN POSITION FROM #1 (EXAMPLE: ARROGANCE, NERDINESS, DIMNESS, ETC.)	2 _____
YOUR POSITION IN THE OFFICE	3 _____
BODY PART	4 _____
OCCUPATION	5 _____
AN EVENT/ACTIVITY #1 MIGHT ATTEND	6 _____
ANOTHER EVENT/ACTIVITY #1 MIGHT ATTEND	7 _____
ANOTHER EVENT/ACTIVITY #1 MIGHT ATTEND	8 _____
#1 (PLURAL)	9 _____
ITEM #1 USES AT WORK	10 _____
ANOTHER ITEM #1 USES AT WORK	11 _____
SYNONYM FOR "USE" (PAST TENSE)	12 _____
POSITION FROM #1	13 _____
POSITION FROM #1	14 _____

"There is reason in an 1_____, though nature has made him

with 2_____!" said the 3_____, shaking

his 4_____ like one whom such an appeal to his justice was

not thrown away. For a moment he appeared to be conscious of having

the worst of the argument, then rallying again, he answered the objec-

tion of his antagonist in the best manner his limited information would

allow: "I am no 5_____, and I care not who knows it;

but judging from what I have seen, as 6_____ and

7_____, of the 8_____, I think a rifle in the hands

of 9_____was not so dangerous as a 10_____

and a good 11_____ might be, if 12_____

with 13_____ judgment, and sent by a(n)

14_____ eye."

Bram Stoker's Sesame Street

"It was horrible. Horrible, I tell you! The creature slowly rose from its coffin and lurched toward me. I brandished my cross and stake, but to no avail! And that's when it happened. The creature...the creature... LICKED MY FACE! OH, THE HORROR!"

OK, so maybe that's not how Bram Stoker's *Dracula* goes, but it's amazing how by changing a few words around you can go from a villainous, bloodsucking monster from Transylvania to a warm, fuzzy monster from a PBS kid's show.

ADJECTIVE TO DESCRIBE SOMETHING CUTE	1	_____
SOUND A SMALL ANIMAL MIGHT MAKE	2	_____
A CUTE ANIMAL	3	_____
ADJECTIVE	4	_____
ADJECTIVE	5	_____
NOUN: SOMETHING SWEET (PLURAL)	6	_____
ADJECTIVE	7	_____
ADJECTIVE	8	_____
ADJECTIVE TO DESCRIBE A CARTOON	9	_____
ADJECTIVE TO DESCRIBE A CUTE ANIMAL	10	_____
SYNONYM FOR "PRANCED"	11	_____
SYNONYM FOR "SWEET"	12	_____
PIECE OF CANDY	13	_____
"CUTE" ADVERB	14	_____
VERB (ENDING IN -ING)	15	_____
A CUTE ANIMAL OR CARTOON	16	_____
AN OBJECT #16 MIGHT ENJOY	17	_____

When Lucy, I call the thing that was before us Lucy because it bore her shape, saw us she drew back with an 1_____ 2_____, such as a(n) 3_____ gives when 4_____, then her eyes ranged over us. Lucy's eyes in form and color, but Lucy's eyes 5_____ and full of 6_____, instead of the pure 7_____ orbs we knew. At the moment the remnant of my love passed into 8_____ loathing. Had she then to be killed, I could have done it with savage delight. As she looked, her eyes blazed with unholy 9_____, and the face became wreathed with a 10_____ smile. Oh, God, how it made me shudder to see it! With a careless motion, she 11_____ to the ground, 12_____ as a devil, the 13_____ that up to now she had clutched 14_____ to her breast 15_____ over it as a 16_____ growls over a 17_____.

I'm not a playa,
I just Middlemarch a lot

Oh, ladies, men are like buses, aren't they? If you miss one, not to worry, there's always another one coming. But what happens when two are coming your way at the same time? Do you get on the local to Maturity-and-Responsibilityville? Or do you beeline for the express to Horneytown?* Help Dorothea from George Eliot's *Middlemarch* solve this age-old dilemma by filling in the blanks.

SLANG FOR HAVING SEX	1	_____
DIRTY MALE BODY PART	2	_____
ANOTHER DIRTY MALE BODY PART	3	_____
FIRST NAME FOR A BORING GUY	4	_____
NAME OF A MALE PORN STAR	5	_____
NAME FROM #4	6	_____
A BORING OCCUPATION	7	_____
A BORING VOLUNTEER POSITION	8	_____
A PERSON ENGAGING IN A BORING HOBBY (EXAMPLE: DOOR PAINTER, ROCK COLLECTOR, ETC.)	9	_____
NAME FROM #5	10	_____
NAME FROM #5	11	_____
SLANG FOR "LOVER"	12	_____
PET NAME FOR A LOVER	13	_____
THE HOBBY FROM #9 EXPRESSED AS A VERB (EXAMPLE: PAINTER, PAINTING OR COLLECTOR, COLLECTING)	14	_____
NAME FROM #5	15	_____
MALE BODY PART (PLURAL)	16	_____
SLANG FOR HAVING SEX	17	_____

*IT'S A REAL TOWN IN NORTH CAROLINA. LOOK IT UP.

"Well, you are not fond of 1_____, a great 2_____, balls, 3_____, that kind of thing. I can see that 4_____'s ways might suit you better than 5_____'s. And you shall do as you like my dear. I would not hinder 6_____; I said so at once; for there is no knowing how anything may turn out. You have not the same tastes as every young lady; and a 7_____ and 8_____—who may be a 9_____—that kind of thing—may suit you better than 10_____. 11_____ is a good 12_____, a good sound-hearted 13_____, you know; but he doesn't go much into 14_____. I did, when I was his age. But 15_____'s 16_____, no. I think he has hurt them a little with too much 17_____."

Henry James, Classic New Yorker

Henry James, your mastery of English is just so … so … *English.* So proper. So reserved. Your prose in *The Portrait of a Lady*, with all of its delightfully buoyant British-ness, is no exception. But, as we all know, the English and the Americans are divided by a common language. So, for our Yank readers, read this passage in a thick New York accent. And please, enjoy filling out this passage tentatively entitled *Portrait of a Broad I Made Out with Once at Cousin Jimmy's Cookout in Newark.*

SLANG FOR "COOL"	1	_____
AN EVENT NEW YORKERS MIGHT PARTAKE IN	2	_____
A NOUN RELATED TO THE EVENT IN #2	3	_____
SLANG FOR "GREAT"	4	_____
AREA INSIDE A DWELLING	5	_____
NEIGHBORHOOD IN NEW YORK	6	_____
A TYPE OF DWELLING (EXAMPLE: HOUSE. APARTMENT. CONDO. ETC.)	7	_____
SYNONYM FOR "AWESOME"	8	_____
BRAND OF BEER	9	_____
VERB (PAST TENSE. SYNONYM FOR "GONE")	10	_____
A FAMOUS NEW YORKER	11	_____
A TYPE OF PERSON IN NEW YORK (PLURAL)	12	_____
SYNONYM FOR "ARRIVE"	13	_____
ANOTHER TYPE OF NEW YORKER (PLURAL)	14	_____
ADJECTIVE	15	_____
TYPE OF PIZZA (PLURAL)	16	_____
VERB (RELATED TO TEMPERATURE. ENDING IN —ING)	17	_____
A SURFACE WHERE YOU MIGHT PUT FOOD	18	_____

Under certain circumstances there are few hours in life more

1_____ than the hour dedicated to the ceremony known

as 2_____. There are circumstances in which, whether

you partake of the 3_____ or not—some people of course

never do—the situation is in itself 4_____.

Those that I have in mind in beginning to unfold this simple history

offered an admirable setting to an innocent pastime. The implements of

the little feat had been disposed upon the 5_____ of an old

6_____ 7_____, in what I should

call the perfect middle of a 8_____ summer afternoon.

Part of the 9_____ had 10_____, but

much of it was left, and what was left was of the finest and rarest quality.

11_____ would not arrive for many hours; but the flood of

12_____ had begun to 13_____,

the 14_____ had grown 15_____, the

16_____ were 17_____ upon the smooth,

dense 18_____.

Jerry Springer's Guest Host: Jane Eyre!

Hey, have you been watching Jerry Springer recently? Man, that s#!t is bananas! I saw this one about a midget family who runs a cathouse. Then I saw one about these women who rob sex shops and give out what they steal to poor people in the projects. Then I saw this really f#*king crazy s#!t where a guy kept his crazy-a$$ wife locked up in the attic, and then she burned down the house! Oh wait, that wasn't Jerry Springer. That was *Jane Eyre* by Charlotte Brontë. It's still really f#*ked though. Fill in the blanks to see how f#*ked it is.

SCANDALOUS ADVERB	1	_____
ANOTHER SCANDALOUS ADVERB	2	_____
A STREET IN YOUR NEIGHBORHOOD	3	_____
SLANG FOR "CRAZY PERSON"	4	_____
TYPE OF PERSON YOU WOULD SEE ON JERRY SPRINGER	5	_____
ANOTHER TYPE OF PERSON ON JERRY SPRINGER	6	_____
A NUMBER	7	_____
A UNIT OF TIME (PLURAL)	8	_____
A NAME OF SOMEONE YOU MIGHT SEE ON JERRY SPRINGER	9	_____
ADJECTIVE	10	_____
BODY PART (PLURAL)	11	_____
NAME FROM #9	12	_____
SLANG FOR "CRAZY"	13	_____
ANOTHER SLANG WORD FOR "CRAZY"	14	_____
TYPE OF PEOPLE ON JERRY SPRINGER (PLURAL)	15	_____
ANOTHER TYPE OF PEOPLE ON JERRY SPRINGER (PLURAL)	16	_____
A FAMOUS DOCTOR	17	_____

Mr. Rochester continued 1_____ and 2_____ . . .

"I have been married; the woman to whom I was married lives!

You say you never heard of a Mrs. Rochester at the house up

3_____: but I dare say you have many a time inclined

your ear to gossip about the mysterious 4_____ kept

there under watch and ward. Some have whispered to you that she is my

5_____: some my cast-off 6_____; I now

inform you that she is my wife, whom I married 7_____

8_____ ago—9_____

by name, sister of this resolute personage, who is now, with his

10_____ limbs and white 11_____, showing

you what a stout heart men may bear . . . 12_____ is

13_____; and she came of a 14_____

family; 15_____ and 16_____ through

three generations! . . . I had a charming partner—pure, wise,

modest: you can fancy I was a happy man . . . But I owe you no

further explanation—I invite you all to come up to the house and

visit 17_____'s patient, and *my wife!*"

Portrait of the Artist with Bad Judgment

This has happened to all of us: A friend won't stop talking about their new boyfriend or girlfriend and how gorgeous, funny, and smart they are. Then you finally meet your friend's new significant other, who is about as attractive as one of those weird hairless cats, and you think: "Well, two out of three ain't bad."

To flip through James Joyce's Guinness-soaked biography, one might guess he's no exception. Some of his hotties were undoubtedly viewed through beer goggles. Fill in the blanks for this passage from *A Portrait of the Artist as a Young Man* to discover a girl who, um, has a great personality.

NAME OF A GROCERY STORE	1	_____
AN AISLE IN THAT GROCERY STORE	2	_____
A DEPRESSING CITY	3	_____
ADJECTIVE	4	_____
ADJECTIVE	5	_____
UNATTRACTIVE ANIMAL	6	_____
ADJECTIVE	7	_____
ADJECTIVE	8	_____
A LARGE ANIMAL	9	_____
COLOR	10	_____
FOOD THAT IS THE SAME COLOR AS #10	11	_____
A SOFT, SLIGHTLY LIQUID FOOD	12	_____
SLANG TERM FOR "UNDERWEAR"	13	_____
A ROUGH BUILDING MATERIAL	14	_____
A GROSS COLOR	15	_____
BODY PART	16	_____
ANIMAL	17	_____
ADJECTIVE	18	_____
ADJECTIVE	19	_____
ADJECTIVE	20	_____
AN UNATTRACTIVE CELEBRITY	21	_____

A girl stood before him in 1_____: alone and still,

gazing out to 2_____. She seemed like one

whom 3_____ had changed into the likeness of a

4_____ and 5_____ 6_____.

Her 7_____ 8_____ bare legs were delicate as

a 9_____'s and pure save where a(n) 10_____

trail of 11_____ had fashioned itself as a sign upon the

flesh. Her thighs fuller and soft-hued as 12_____,

were bared almost to the hips where the white fringes of her

13_____ were like feathering of soft white

14_____. Her 15_____ skirts were

kilted boldly about her 16_____ and dovetailed behind

her. Her bosom was a 17_____'s, 18_____

and 19_____, 20_____ and soft as the breast

of 21_____.

Poor fashion choices: a cardinal sin

Hester Prynne in *The Scarlet Letter* is ostracized and cast out for committing the act of adultery. But that was almost 400 years ago. Ask the cast of *Mad Men*, or any of the 500 million people who visit Japanese "love hotels"…adultery just doesn't turn heads the way it used to. Now, if you want to be shunned, if you want to be exiled, if you want to be excommunicated, then you need to commit a much greater sin…. *wearing an outfit that is soooo last season.*

SYNONYM FOR "OWNER"	1	_____
PHRASE FOR SOMETHING REALLY BAD (EXAMPLE: CATASTROPHE. FAUX PAS. CLUSTERF#$K)	2	_____
RESTAURANT IN A MALL FOOD COURT	3	_____
AN ITEM OR ACCESSORY THAT IS WAY OUT OF STYLE	4	_____
BODY PART	5	_____
SYNONYM FOR "COOLNESS"	6	_____
A FASHION ACCESSORY THAT IS OUT OF STYLE	7	_____
AN ARTICLE OF CLOTHING (FOR YOUR UPPER BODY) THAT IS OUT OF STYLE	8	_____
ITEM FROM #4	9	_____
TYPE OF PERSON YOU WOULD SEE IN A MALL (PLURAL)	10	_____
ANOTHER TYPE OF PERSON YOU WOULD SEE IN A MALL (PLURAL)	11	_____
ITEM IN #8	12	_____
ADJECTIVE MEANING "UNCOOL"	13	_____
LOGO OF A BRAND THAT IS NO LONGER POPULAR	14	_____

When the young woman—the 1_____ of this

2_____—stood fully revealed before the

3_____, it seemed to be her first impulse to clasp the

4_____ closely to her 5_____; not so

much by an impulse of 6_____, as that she might

thereby conceal a certain 7_____, which was

wrought or fastened into her 8_____. In a moment,

however wisely judging that one token of her shame would but poorly

serve to hide another, she took the 9_____ on her arm,

and, with a burning blush, and yet a haughty smile and a glance that

would not be abashed, looked around her 10_____ and

11_____. On the breast of her 12_____,

in fine red cloth, surrounded with an elaborate embroidery and fantastic

flourishes of gold thread, appeared the 13_____

14_____.

The (Rude) Awakening

Ever been to a wedding where someone in the row behind you whispers "it won't last"? And you know it, too. Everyone at the wedding knows it. It's so obvious. She's a social butterfly, he's a devastating introvert. He likes camping, and she's a real city slicker. She's really, really into *Star Trek* and anime, and he's...well...really, really not. There are a lot of signs that some lovebirds just can't see. Edna in *The Awakening* should have seen that her marriage was a bad idea, but she didn't. So, to help her out, fill in all the reasons why it's a bad idea for her.

NAME FOR A MALE PET	1	_____
ADJECTIVE	2	_____
PET STORE CHAIN	3	_____
A TYPE OF EVENT/PARTY	4	_____
SYNONYM FOR "PET"/"ANIMAL" (PLURAL)	5	_____
VERB (PAST TENSE, SOMETHING A DOG CAN DO)	6	_____
THING DOGS LIKE	7	_____
ANOTHER THING DOGS LIKE (PLURAL)	8	_____
OCCUPATION	9	_____
BREED OF DOG	10	_____
PET NAME FROM #1	11	_____

Her marriage to 1_____ was purely 2_____, in this respect resembling many other marriages which masquerade as the decrees of 3_____. It was in the midst of her secret 4_____ that she met him. He fell in love, as 5_____ are in the habit of doing, and 6_____ his 7_____ with an earnestness and an ardor which left nothing to be desired. He pleased her; his absolute devotion flattered her. She fancied there was a sympathy of thought and 8_____ between them, in which fancy she was mistaken. Add to this the violent opposition of her father and her 9_____ to her marriage with a 10_____, and we need see no further for the motives which led her to accept 11_____ for her husband.

AS Interesting AS Watching Trees Grow

Poor Joyce Kilmer, you were killed too young in the Great War. Now, the most famous poem we have of yours is "Trees." It's about how the most beautiful thing you ever saw was a tree. To see such young talent write of such things, it makes one think...that you probably should have gone out more. The most beautiful thing *ever* is a tree? Seriously? Read some more about how Joyce Kilmer loved boring things by filling in the blanks.

A BORING. MANMADE THING	1	_____
BORING THING FROM #1	2	_____
ADJECTIVE	3	_____
BODY PART	4	_____
AN UNATTRACTIVE FEMALE CELEBRITY	5	_____
BORING THING FROM #1	6	_____
A BORING TELEVISION SHOW	7	_____
ADJECTIVE	8	_____
PART OF THE BORING THING FROM #1	9	_____
BORING THING FROM #1	10	_____
AN UGLY TYPE OF HAT	11	_____
ANOTHER PART OF THE BORING ITEM FROM #1	12	_____
A TYPE OF PACKING MATERIAL	13	_____
SOMETHING THAT WOULD SURROUND THE BORING ITEM FROM #1	14	_____
STORE WHERE YOU BUY #1	15	_____
ITEM FROM #1	16	_____

I THINK that I shall never see

A poem lovely as a <u>1   </u>.

A <u>2   </u> whose <u>3   </u>

   <u>4   </u> is prest

Against <u>5   </u>'s flowing breast;

A <u>6   </u> that looks at <u>7   </u> all day,

And lifts her <u>8   </u> <u>9   </u> to pray;

A <u>10   </u> that may in summer wear

A <u>11   </u> in her hair;

Upon whose <u>12   </u> <u>13   </u> has lain;

Who intimately lives with <u>14   </u>.

Poems are made by fools like me,

But only <u>15   </u> can make a <u>16   </u>.

Oliver Twist by Charles ^the^ Dickens

Charles Dickens had a soft spot for orphans, and nowhere is this more exemplified than in *Oliver Twist*. Oliver is a sweet, polite, good-natured kid who's been dealt a bad hand. But not all kids are like this. Some kids are mean. Some kids would pick your pocket even if they didn't have to. Some kids know how to make shivs. I hate to break it to you, gentle reader, but some kids are little s#!ts. Fill in the blanks to meet the Oliver Twist who deserved to be dealt a bad hand.

APPLIANCE USED FOR COOKING	1	_____
ADJECTIVE	2	_____
YOUR FAVORITE FOOD	3	_____
A CHAIN RESTAURANT	4	_____
FOOD FROM #3	5	_____
VERB (A FRIENDLY GESTURE, PAST TENSE)	6	_____
VERB (FRIENDLY, PAST TENSE)	7	_____
ADJECTIVE TO DESCRIBE A JERK	8	_____
CHARACTERISTIC OF A JERK (EXAMPLE: ARROGANCE, ANGER, INCONSIDERATION, ETC.)	9	_____
ANOTHER ADJECTIVE TO DESCRIBE A JERK	10	_____
ANOTHER CHARACTERISTIC OF A JERK	11	_____
AN IMPROVISED WEAPON (EXAMPLE: A BROKEN BOTTLE, A BASEBALL BAT)	12	_____
ANOTHER IMPROVISED WEAPON	13	_____
SYNONYM FOR "PLEASED"	14	_____
CHARACTERISTIC OF A DANGEROUS MAN	15	_____
A QUICK, COMMON, PROFANE PHRASE	16	_____
SYNONYM FOR "NICE"	17	_____
SYNONYM FOR "FRIENDLY"	18	_____
APPLIANCE FROM #1	19	_____
PHRASE FROM #16	20	_____

The evening arrived; the boys took their places. The master, in his cook's uniform, stationed himself at the 1_____; his 2_____ assistants ranged themselves behind him; the 3_____ was served out; and long grace was said over the 4_____. The 5_____ disappeared; the boys whispered to each other, and 6_____ at Oliver; while his next neighbors 7_____ him. Child as he was, he was 8_____ with 9_____, and 10_____ with 11_____. He rose from the table; and advancing to the master, 12_____ and 13_____ in hand, said, somewhat 14_____ at his own 15_____—

"16_____, sir, I want some more."

The master was a 17_____, 18_____ man; but he turned very pale. He gazed in stupefied astonishment on the small rebel for some seconds; and then clung for support to the 19_____. The assistants were paralyzed with wonder; the boys with fear.

"What!" said the master at length, in faint voice.

"20_____, sir," replied Oliver, "I want some more."

Huck Finn: Dork on a Raft

In Mark Twain's *The Adventures of Tom Sawyer*, Huckleberry Finn is
painted as a rebel, a wayward kid, and a bad boy whom no mother would
want her son to hang around with. And it's true, mothers don't like
their kids hanging out with bad boys. But there's another group mothers don't like seeing their sons hang with: nerds. Who wants a kid who
misses the Homecoming party to stay in and play *World of Warcraft*?
Or who turns in a science project titled *Several Attempts at Getting
Female Humans to Kiss Me*? Fill in the blanks to see how Huck Finn
would be different if he was a dork instead of a daredevil.

A VERY NERDY PROFESSION	1	_____
ADJECTIVE TO DESCRIBE A DORK	2	_____
ANOTHER ADJECTIVE TO DESCRIBE A DORK	3	_____
ANOTHER ADJECTIVE TO DESCRIBE A DORK	4	_____
ANOTHER ADJECTIVE TO DESCRIBE A DORK	5	_____
AN ITEM A NERDY KID WOULD PLAY WITH	6	_____
A LARGE PIECE OF SCIENTIFIC EQUIPMENT	7	_____
AN INDOOR PLACE A NERD WOULD VISIT	8	_____
A PLACE POPULAR KIDS HANG OUT	9	_____
ANOTHER PLACE POPULAR KIDS HANG OUT	10	_____
A NICKNAME COOL KIDS CALL EACH OTHER	11	_____
A TYPE OF COOL KID (PLURAL)	12	_____
VERB (A NERD ACTIVITY, ENDING IN –ING)	13	_____
ANOTHER NERD ACTIVITY (ENDING IN –ING)	14	_____
A GEEKY VERB	15	_____
A VERY UNCOOL TYPE OF SHOE (PLURAL)	16	_____
VERB (THING COOL KIDS DO)	17	_____
A HIP ARTICLE OF CLOTHING (PLURAL)	18	_____
VERB (THING NERDS DO)	19	_____
NAME OF A CITY	20	_____

Shortly Tom came upon the juvenile pariah of the village, Huckleberry Finn, son of the town 1_____. Huckleberry was cordially hated and dreaded by all the mothers of the town, because he was

2_____ and 3_____ and 4_____ and

5_____—and because all their children admired him so, and delighted in his 6_____, and wished they dared to be like him. Tom was like the rest of the respectable boys, in that he envied Huckleberry his gaudy outcast condition, and was under strict orders not to play with him. So he played with him every time he got a chance. . . .

Huckleberry came and went, at his own free will. He slept on

7_____ in fine weather and in empty 8_____ in wet; he did not have to go to 9_____ or to 10_____, or call any being 11_____ or obey 12_____; he could go 13_____ or 14_____ when and where he chose, and stay as long as it suited him; nobody forbade him to 15_____; he could sit up as late as he pleased; he was always the first boy that went barefoot in the spring and the last to resume 16_____ in the fall; he never had to 17_____, nor put on 18_____; he could 19_____ wonderfully. In a word, everything that goes to make life precious that boy had. So thought every harassed, hampered, respectable boy in 20_____.

By the author of Coriolanus

If there's one thing we can learn from R-rated movies, shows on HBO, and the lexicon of Samuel L. Jackson, it's this: people like it when you say motherf#@ker. A good showman knows that, whether rain, snow, or shine, incessant and unyielding profanity puts butts in seats. So then why didn't Shakespeare, arguably one of our greatest showmen, use four-letter words? Well, he did. But back then they were ten-letter words. So, if a little vocabulary overhaul is all it takes to get modern folks to read the bard, far be it for us to stand in the f#@king way. Fill in the blanks to update this swear-happy passage from *King Lear*, then go wash your mouth out with soap.

A PROFANE NAME TO CALL SOMEONE	1	_____
ADJECTIVE	2	_____
BODY PART (PLURAL)	3	_____
PROFANE ADJECTIVE	4	_____
ANOTHER BODY PART	5	_____
A BIG NUMBER	6	_____
DIRTY ADJECTIVE	7	_____
ARTICLE OF CLOTHING	8	_____
NOUN	9	_____
AN OCCUPATION HELD BY AN OLD WOMAN	10	_____
NOUN	11	_____
A DIRTY NAME TO CALL SOMEONE	12	_____
ADJECTIVE	13	_____
A DIRTY WORD	14	_____
ANIMAL	15	_____
SOMEONE YOU WOULD NOT WANT TO BE EMBARRASSED IN FRONT OF	16	_____
ADJECTIVE	17	_____
A DIRTY WORD	18	_____

OSWALD: Why dost thou use me thus? I know thee not.

KENT: 1_____, I know thee.

OSWALD: What dost thou know me for?

KENT: A knave; a rascal; an eater of 2_____
3_____; a 4_____, proud, shallow, beggarly, three-5_____ed, 6_____-pound, filthy, 7_____-8_____ knave; a lily-livered, 9_____-taking whoreson, 10_____-gazing, super-serviceable, finical rogue; one-11_____-inheriting slave; one that wouldst be a 12_____, in way of good service, and art nothing but the composition of a knave, beggar, coward, pander, and the son and heir of a mongrel bitch: one whom I will beat into clamorous whining, if thou deniest the least syllable of thy addition.

OSWALD: Why what a 13_____ fellow art thou, thus to rail on one that is neither known of thee nor knows thee!

KENT: What a 14_____-faced 15_____ art thou, to deny thou knowest me! It is two days ago since I tripped up thy heels, and beat thee before 16_____? Draw, you rogue: for though it be night, yet the moon shines; I'll make a sop o' the moonshine of you: draw, you 17_____ 18_____monger, draw.

Treasure Television Island

And now, an excerpt from little Billy Ford's book report on Robert Louis Stevenson's *Treasure Island.*

> "When running from the Dharma Initiative on the island, Jim Hawkins runs into a professor who can make a radio out of coconuts. They decide who will vote them off the island. Then Captain Jack Sparrow comes and they have a party."

Ok, so it's clear that Billy didn't read *Treasure Island*. But who can blame him, especially when *Lost, Survivor, Gilligan's Island,* and *Pirates of the Caribbean* are all on TV? To see the book Billy wishes he'd read, fill in the blanks with a character from one of these shows in mind. Feel free to use another show or movie!

MALE CHARACTER FROM A SHIPWRECK MOVIE OR TV SHOW	1	_____
ADJECTIVE TO DESCRIBE THIS CHARACTER	2	_____
ANOTHER ADJECTIVE TO DESCRIBE THIS CHARACTER	3	_____
ANOTHER ADJECTIVE TO DESCRIBE THIS CHARACTER	4	_____
ANIMAL	5	_____
NAME FROM #1	6	_____
ANOTHER CHARACTER FROM THIS MOVIE OR TV SHOW	7	_____
OCCUPATION OF THIS CHARACTER	8	_____
VERB (PAST TENSE)	9	_____
BODY PART	10	_____
COLOR	11	_____
ADJECTIVE TO DESCRIBE THIS CHARACTER	12	_____
OCCUPATION FROM #8	13	_____
BODY PART	14	_____
ARTICLE OF CLOTHING THIS CHARACTER MIGHT WEAR	15	_____
ITEM THIS CHARACTER MIGHT LIKE	16	_____
ITEM FROM #16	17	_____
ITEM FROM #16	18	_____

"Who are you?" I asked.

"1_____," he answered, and his voice sounded 2_____ and 3_____, like a 4_____ 5_____. "I'm poor 6_____, I am; and I haven't spoke with 7_____ these three years."

I could now see that he was a 8_____ like myself, and that his features were even pleasing. His skin, wherever it was exposed, was 9_____ by the sun; even his 10_____ were 11_____; and his fair eyes looked quite startling in so 12_____ a face. Of all the 13_____ that I had seen or fancied, he was the chief for raggedness. . . . About his 14_____ he wore an old 15_____, which was the thing solid in his whole accoutrement.

"Three years!" I cried. "Were you shipwrecked?"

"Nay, mate," said he—"marooned.". . . .

"Marooned three years agone," he continued, "and lived on goats since then, and berries, and oysters. Wherever a man is, says I, a man can do for himself. But, mate, my heart is sore for 16_____. You mightn't happen to have a piece of 17_____ about you, now? No? Well, many's the long night I've dreamed of 18_____—toasted, mostly— and woke up again, and here I were."

Aesop's Fables, by Aesop

AN ASS, belonging to an herb-seller who gave him too little food and too much work made a petition to Jupiter to be released from his present service and provided with another master. Jupiter, after warning him that he would repent his request, caused him to be sold to a tile-maker. Shortly afterwards, finding that he had heavier loads to carry and harder work in the brick-field, he petitioned for another change of master. Jupiter, telling him that it would be the last time that he could grant his request, ordained that he be sold to a tanner. The Ass found that he had fallen into worse hands, and noting his master's occupation, said, groaning: "It would have been better for me to have been either starved by the one, or to have been overworked by the other of my former masters, than to have been bought by my present owner . . ."

Little Women, by Louisa May Alcott

Margaret seemed to find it a little hard to tell hers, and waved a brake before her face, as if to disperse imaginary gnats while she said slowly, "I should like a lovely house, full of all sorts of luxurious things—nice food, pretty clothes, handsome furniture, pleasant people, and heaps of money. I am to be mistress of it, and manage it as I like, with plenty of servants, so I never need to work a bit. How I should enjoy it! For I wouldn't be idle, but do good, and make everyone love me dearly."

. . . "Why don't you say you'd have a splendid, wise, good husband and some angelic little children? You know your castle wouldn't be perfect without," said blunt Jo, who had no tender fancies yet, and rather scorned romance, except in books.

"You'd have nothing but horses, inkstands, and novels in yours," answered Meg petulantly.

"Wouldn't I though? I have a stable full of Arabian steeds, rooms piled high with books, and I'd write out of a magic inkstand, so that my works should be as famous as Laurie's music."

. . . "Mine is to stay at home safe with Father and Mother, and help take care of the family," said Beth contentedly.

Emma, by Jane Austen

Human nature is so well disposed towards those who are in interesting situations that a young person who either marries or dies is sure of being kindly spoken of.

A week had not passed since Miss Hawkins's name was first mentioned in Highbury, before she was, by some means or other, discovered to have every recommendation of person and mind—to be handsome, elegant, highly accomplished, and perfectly amiable; and when Mr. Elton himself arrived to triumph in his happy prospects and circulate the fame of her merits, there was very little more for him to do than to tell her Christian name, and say whose musical she principally played. . . .

The charming Augusta Hawkins, in addition to all the usual advantages of perfect beauty and merit, was in possession of an independent fortune of so many thousands as would always be called ten—a point of some dignity, as well as some convenience.

Pride and Prejudice, by Jane Austen

R eally, Mr. Collins," cried Elizabeth, with some warmth, "you puzzle me exceedingly. If what I have hitherto said can appear to you in the form of encouragement, I know not how to express my refusal in such a way as may convince you of its being one."

"You must give me leave to flatter myself, my dear cousin, that your refusal of my addresses are merely words of course. . . . It does not appear to me that my hand is unworthy of your acceptance, or that the establishment I can offer would be any other than highly desirable. My situation in life, my connections with the family of De Bourge, and my relationship to your own, are the circumstances highly in my favor; and you should take it into further consideration that, in spite of your manifold attractions, it is by no means certain that another offer of marriage may ever be made to you. . . . As I must, therefore, conclude that you are not serious in your rejection of me. I shall choose to attribute it to your wish of increasing my love by suspense, according to the usual practice of all elegant females."

Peter Pan, by J. M. Barrie

"I t was because I heard father and mother," he explained in a low voice, "talking about what I was to be when I became a man." He was extraordinarily agitated now. "I don't want ever to be a man," he said with passion. "I want always to be a little boy and to have fun. So I ran away to Kensington Gardens and lived a long, long time among the fairies."

She gave him a look of the most intense admiration, and he thought it was because he had run away, but it was really because he knew fairies. Wendy had lived such a home life that to know fairies struck her as quite delightful. She poured out questions about them, to his surprise, for they were rather nuisance to him, getting in his way and so on, and indeed he sometimes had to give them a hiding. Still, he liked them on the whole, and he told her about the beginning of fairies.

"You see, Wendy, when the first baby laughed for the first time, its laugh broke into a thousand pieces, and they all went skipping about, and that was the beginning of fairies."

The Wonderful Wizard of Oz, by L. Frank Baum

B ut what interested Dorothy most was the big throne of green marble that stood in the middle of the room. It was shaped like a chair and sparkled with gems, as did everything else. In the center of the chair was an enormous Head, without a body to support it or any arms or legs whatever. There was no hair upon his head, but it had eyes and a nose and a mouth, and was much bigger than the head of the biggest giant.

As Dorothy gazed upon this in wonder and fear, the eyes turned slowly and looked at her sharply and steadily. Then the mouth moved, and Dorothy heard a voice say:

"I am Oz, the Great and Terrible. Who are you and why do you seek me?"

It was not such an awful voice as she expected to come from the big head; so she took courage and answered:

"I am Dorothy, the Small and Meek. I have come to you for help."

"The Tiger," by William Blake

TIGER, tiger, burning bright
In the forests of the night,
What immortal hand or eye
Could frame thy fearful symmetry?

In what distant deeps or skies
Burnt the fire of thine eyes?
On what wings dare he aspire?
What the hand dare seize the fire?

When the stars threw down their spears,
And water'd heaven with their tears,
Did He smile His work to see?
Did He who made the lamb make thee?

Tiger, tiger, burning bright
In the forests of the night,
What immortal hand or eye
Dare frame thy fearful symmetry?

Jane Eyre, by Charlotte Brontë

Mr. Rochester continued hardily and recklessly . . . "I have been married; the woman to whom I was married lives! You say you never heard of a Mrs. Rochester at the house up yonder, Wood: but I dare say you have many a time inclined your ear to gossip about the mysterious lunatic kept there under watch and ward. Some have whispered to you that she is my bastard half-sister, some my cast-off mistress; I now inform you that she is my wife, whom I married fifteen years ago—Bertha Mason by name, sister of this resolute personage, who is now, with his quivering limbs and white cheeks, showing you what a stout heart men may bear . . . Bertha Mason is mad; and she came of a mad family; idiots and maniacs through three generations! . . . I had a charming partner—pure, wise, modest: you can fancy I was a happy man . . . But I owe you no further explanation. Briggs, Wood, Mason—I invite you all to come up to the house and visit Mrs. Poole's patient, and *my wife!*"

Wuthering Heights, by Emily Brontë

"This is nothing," cried she: "I was only going to say that heaven did not seem to be my home; and I broke my heart with weeping to come back to earth; and the angels were so angry that they flung me out into the middle of the heath on top of Wuthering Heights; where I woke sobbing for joy. That will do to explain my secret, as well as the other. I've no more business to marry Edgar Linton than I have to be in heaven; and if the wicked man in there had not brought Heathcliff so low, I shouldn't have thought of it. It would degrade me to marry Heathcliff now; so he shall never know how I love him: and that, not because he's handsome, Nelly, but because he's more myself than I am. Whatever our souls are made of, his and mine are the same; and Linton's is as different as a moonbeam from lightning, or frost from fire."

Tarzan King of the Apes, by Edgar Rice Burroughs

While he waited he passed the time printing a message to her; whether he intended giving it to her he himself could not have told, but he took infinite pleasure in seeing his thoughts expressed in print—in which he was not so uncivilized after all. He wrote:

I am Tarzan of the Apes. I want you. I am yours. You are mine. We will live here together always in my house. I will bring you the best fruits, and the tenderest deer, the finest meats that roam the jungle. I will hunt for you. I am the greatest of the jungle hunters. I will fight for you. I am the mightiest of the jungle fighters. You are Jane Porter, I saw it in your letter. When you see this you will know that it is for you and that Tarzan of the Apes loves you.

As he stood, straight as a young Indian, by the door, waiting after he had finished the message, there came to his keen ears a familiar sound. It was the passing of a great ape through the lower branches of the forest.

For an instant he listened intently, and then from the jungle came the agonized scream of a woman, and Tarzan of the Apes, dropping his first love letter upon the ground, shot like a panther into the forest.

Alice's Adventures in Wonderland, by Lewis Carroll

"In that direction," the Cat said, waving its right paw round, "lives a Hatter: and in that direction," waving the other paw, "lives a March Hare. Visit either you like: they're both mad."

"But I don't want to go among mad people," Alice remarked.

"Oh, you can't help that," said the Cat: "we're all mad here. I'm mad. You're mad."

"How do you know I'm mad?" said Alice.

"You must be," said the Cat, "or you wouldn't have come here."

Alice didn't think that proved it at all: however, she went on: "And how do you know that you're mad?"

"To begin with," said the Cat, "a dog's not mad. You grant that?"

"I suppose so," said Alice.

"Well, then," the Cat went on, "you see a dog growls when it's angry, and wags its tail when it's pleased. Now I growl when I'm pleased, and wag my tail when I'm angry. Therefore I'm mad."

"I call it purring not growling," said Alice.

"Call it what you like," said the Cat.

The Awakening, by Kate Chopin

Her marriage to Leonce Pontellier was purely an accident, in this respect resembling many other marriages which masquerade as the decrees of Fate. It was in the midst of her secret great passion that she met him. He fell in love, as men are in the habit of doing, and pressed his suit with an earnestness and an ardor which left nothing to be desired. He pleased her; his absolute devotion flattered her. She fancied there was a sympathy of thought and taste between them, in which fancy she was mistaken. Add to this the violent opposition of her father and her sister Margaret to her marriage with a Catholic, and we need see no further for the motives which led her to accept Monsieur Pontellier for her husband.

Heart of Darkness, by Joseph Conrad

My first interview with the manager was curious. . . . He was common-place in complexion, in features, in manners, and in voice. He was of middle size and of ordinary build. His eyes, of the usual blue, were perhaps remarkably cold, and he certainly could make his glance fall on one as trenchant and heavy as an ax. But even at these times the rest of his person seemed to disclaim the intention. Otherwise there was only an indefinable, faint expression of his lips, something stealthy—a smile—not a smile—I remember it, but I can't explain. It was unconscious, this smile was though just after he had said something it got intensified for an instant. It came at the end of his speeches like a seal applied on the words to make the meaning of the commonest phrase appear absolutely inscrutable. He was a common trader, from his youth up employed in these parts—nothing more. He was obeyed, yet he inspired neither love nor fear, nor even respect. He inspired uneasiness. That was it! Uneasiness.

The Last of the Mohicans, by James Fenimore Cooper

There is reason in an Indian, though nature has made him with red skin!" said the white man, shaking his head like on whom such an appeal to his justice was not thrown away. For a moment he appeared to be conscious of having the worst of the argument, then rallying again, he answered the objection of his antagonist in the best manner his limited information would allow: "I am no scholar, and I care not who knows it; but judging from what I have seen, as deer chases and squirrel hunts, of the sparks below, I think a rifle in the hands of their grandfathers was not so dangerous as a hickory bow and a good flint-head might be, if drawn with Indian judgment, and sent by an Indian eye."

The Red Badge of Courage, by Stephen Crane

He wished, without reserve, that he was at home again making the endless rounds from the house to the barn, from the barn to the fields, from the fields to the barn, from the barn to the house. He remembered he had often cursed the brindle cow and her mates, and had sometimes flung milking stools. But, from his present point of view, there was a halo of happiness about each of their heads, and he would have sacrificed all the brass buttons on the continent to have been enabled to return to them. He told himself that he was not formed for a soldier. And he mused seriously upon the radical differences between himself and the men who were dodging implike around the fires.

Robinson Crusoe, by Daniel Defoe

I let him know that his name was to be Friday, which was the day on which his life was saved, and I taught him that he was to call me master.

Taking a cup of milk, I drank some of it and moistened my bread in some. I gave Friday a cup of milk; he did the same thing with his bread, showing by signs that he thought it very good. . . .

Friday, after a while, knew English so well that I could talk to him about anything that I wished.

I taught him that there is one God who made everything and that He loves men as a father loves his children, and that He cares for them even more tenderly than does a father. When Christmas time came I taught him about Jesus.

I told him how I happened to be on the island, and how long I had been there and what a hard time I had had at first to get food and make a home, and how lonely I had been until he came.

Great Expectations, by Charles Dickens

You are part of my existence, part of myself. You have been in every line I have ever read, since I first came here, the rough common boy whose poor heart you wounded even then. You have been in every prospect I have ever seen since—on the river, on the sails of the ships, on the marshes, in the clouds, in the light, in the darkness, in the wind, in the woods, in the sea, in the streets. You have been the embodiment of every graceful fancy that my mind has ever become acquainted with. The stones of which the strongest London buildings are made, are not more real, or more impossible to be displaced by your hands, than your presence and influence have been to me, there and everywhere, and will be. Estella, to the last hour of my life, you cannot choose but remain part of my character, part of the little good in me, part of the evil.

Oliver Twist, by Charles Dickens

The evening arrived; the boys took their places. The master, in his cook's uniform, stationed himself at the copper; his pauper assistants ranged themselves behind him; the gruel was served out; and long grace was said over the short commons. The gruel disappeared; the boys whispered to each other, and winked at Oliver; while his next neighbors nudged him. Child as he was, he was desperate with hunger, and reckless with misery. He rose from the table; and advancing to the master, basin and spoon in hand, said, somewhat alarmed at his own temerity—

"Please, sir, I want some more."

The master was a fat, healthy man; but he turned very pale. He gazed in stupefied astonishment on the small rebel for some seconds; and then clung for support to the copper. The assistants were paralyzed with wonder; the boys with fear.

"What!" said the master at length, in faint voice.

"Please, sir," replied Oliver, "I want some more."

"A Bird Came Down the Walk," by Emily Dickenson

A bird came down the walk:
He did not know I saw;
He bit an angle-worm in halves
And ate the fellow, raw.

And then he drank a dew
From a convenient grass,
And then hopped sidewise to the wall
To let a beetle pass.

He glanced with rapid eyes
That hurried all abroad—
They looked like frightened beads, I
    thought;
He stirred his velvet head

Like one in danger; cautious,
I offered him a crumb,
And he unrolled his feathers
And rowed him softer home

Than oars divide the ocean,
Too silver for a seam,
Or butterflies, off banks of noon,
Leap, splashless, as they swim.

A Study in Scarlet: Sherlock Holmes, by Sir Arthur Conan Doyle

Its somewhat ambitious title was "The Book of Life," and it attempted to show how much an observant man might learn by an accurate and systematic examination of all that came in his way. It struck me as being a remarkable mixture of shrewdness and of absurdity. The reasoning was close and intense, but the deductions appeared to me to be far-fetched and exaggerated. . . .

"From a drop of water," said the writer, "a logician could infer the possibility of an Atlantic or a Niagara without having seen or heard of one or the other. So all life is a great chain, the nature of which is known whenever we are shown a single link of it. Like all other arts, the Science of Deduction and Analysis is one which can only be acquired by a long and patient study. . . . By a man's finger nails, by his coat-sleeve, by his boot, by his trouser knees, by the callosities of his forefinger and thumb, by his expression, by his shirt cuffs—by each of these things a man's calling is plainly revealed. That all united should fail to enlighten the competent enquirer in any case is almost inconceivable."

Middlemarch, by George Eliot

"Well, you are not fond of show, a great establishment, balls, dinners, that kind of thing. I can see that Casaubon's ways might suit you better than Chettam's. And you shall do as you like my dear. I would not hinder Casaubon; I said so at once; for there is no knowing how anything may turn out. You have not the same tastes as every young lady; and a clergyman and scholar—who may be a bishop—that kind of thing—may suit you better than Chettam. Chettam is a good fellow, a good sound-hearted fellow, you know; but he doesn't go much into ideas. I did, when I was his age. But Casaubon's eyes, no. I think he has hurt them a little with too much reading."

The Scarlet Letter, by Nathaniel Hawthorne

When the young woman—the mother of this child—stood fully revealed before the crowd, it seemed to be her first impulse to clasp the infant closely to her bosom; not so much by an impulse of motherly affection, as that she might thereby conceal a certain token, which was wrought or fastened into her dress. In a moment, however wisely judging that one token of her shame would but poorly serve to hide another, she took the baby on her arm, and, with a burning blush, and yet a haughty smile and a glance that would not be abashed, looked around her townspeople and neighbors. On the breast of her gown, in fine red cloth, surrounded with an elaborate embroidery and fantastic flourishes of gold thread, appeared the letter A.

The Portrait of a Lady, by Henry James

Under certain circumstances there are few hours in life more agreeable than the hour dedicated to the ceremony known as afternoon tea. There are circumstances in which, whether you partake of the tea or not—some people of course never do—the situation is in itself delightful. Those that I have in mind in beginning to unfold this simple history offered an admirable setting to an innocent pastime. The implements of the little feat had been disposed upon the lawn of an old English country-house, in what I should call the perfect middle of a splendid summer afternoon. Part of the afternoon had waned, but much of it was left, and what was left was of the finest and rarest quality.

Real dusk would not arrive for many hours; but the flood of summer light had begun to ebb, the air had grown mellow, the shadows were long upon the smooth, dense turf.

A Portrait of the Artist as a Young Man, by James Joyce

A girl stood before him in midstream: alone and still, gazing out to sea. She seemed like one whom magic had changed into the likeness of a strange and beautiful seabird. Her long slender bare legs were delicate as a crane's and pure save where an emerald trail of seaweed had fashioned itself as a sign upon the flesh. Her thighs fuller and soft-hued as ivory, were bared almost to the hips where the white fringes of her drawers were like feathering of soft white down. Her slate-blue skirts were kilted boldly about her waist and dovetailed behind her. Her bosom was a bird's, soft and slight, slight and soft as the breast of some dark-plumaged dove.

"Trees," by Joyce Kilmer

I THINK that I shall never see
A poem lovely as a tree.

A tree whose hungry mouth is prest
Against the sweet earth's flowing breast;

A tree that looks at God all day,
And lifts her leafy arms to pray;

A tree that may in summer wear
A nest of robins in her hair;

Upon whose bosom snow has lain;
Who intimately lives with rain.

Poems are made by fools like me,
But only God can make a tree.

Just So Stories, by Rudyard Kipling

The was one Elephant—a new Elephant—an Elephant's child—who was full of 'satiable curiosity, and that means he asked ever so many questions . . . He asked his tall aunt, the Ostrich, why her tail-feathers grew just so, and his tall aunt the Ostrich spanked him with her hard hard claw. He asked his tall uncle the Giraffe, what made his skin spotty, and his tall uncle, the Giraffe, spanked him with his hard, hard hoof. And still he was full of 'satiable curiosity! He asked his broad aunt, the Hippopotamus, why her eyes were red, and his broad aunt, the Hippopotamus, spanked him with her broad, broad hoof; and he asked his hairy uncle, the Baboon, why melons tasted just so, and his hairy uncle the Baboon, spanked him with his hairy hairy paw. And still he was full of 'satiable curiosity.

The Call of the Wild, by Jack London

All day Buck brooded by the pool or roamed restlessly about the camp. . . . At times when he paused to contemplate the carcasses of the Yeehats, he forgot the pain of it; and at such times he was aware of a great pride in himself—a pride greater than any he had yet experienced. He had killed man, the noblest game of all, and he had killed in the face of the law of club and fang. He sniffed the bodies curiously. They had died so easily. It was harder to kill a husky dog than them. They were no match at all, were it not for their arrows and spears and clubs. Thenceforward he would be unafraid of them except when they bore in their hands their arrows, spears, and clubs.

"The Midnight Ride of Paul Revere," by Henry Wadsworth Longfellow

Listen, my children, and you shall hear
Of the midnight ride of Paul Revere,
On the eighteenth of April, in Seventy-five:
Hardly a man is now alive
Who remembers that famous day and year.

He said to his friend, "If the British march
By land or sea from the town to-night,
Hang a lantern aloft in the belfry arch
Of the North Church tower as a signal-light,
One, if by land, and two, if by sea;
And I on the opposite shore will be,
Ready to ride and spread the alarm
Through every Middlesex village and farm,
For the country folk to be up and to arm."

[*Note:* The middle bit was also cut, you know, with all the riding through the night
and warning everyone.]

You know the rest. In the books you have read,
How the British Regulars fired and fled,
How the farmers gave them ball for ball,
From behind each fence and farm-yard wall,
Chasing the red-coats down the lane,
Then crossing the fields to emerge again
Under the trees at the turn of the road,
And only pausing to fire and load.

Moby Dick, by Herman Melville

Call me Ishmael. Some years ago—never mind how long precisely—having little or no money in my purse, and nothing particular to interest me on shore, I thought I would sail about a little and see the watery part of the world. It is a way I have of driving off the spleen, and regulating the circulation. Whenever I find myself growing grim about the mouth; whenever it is a damp, drizzly November in my soul; whenever I find myself involuntarily pausing before coffin warehouses, and bringing up the rear of every funeral I meet; and especially whenever my hypos gets such an upper hand of me, that it requires a strong moral principle to prevent me from deliberately stepping into the street, and methodically knocking people's hats off—then, I account it high time to get to sea as soon as I can.

"The Tell-Tale Heart," by Edgar Allen Poe

It is impossible to say how first the idea entered my brain, but, once conceived, it haunted me day and night. Object there was none. Passion there was none. I loved the old man. He had never wronged me. He had never given me insult. For his gold I had no desire. I think it was his eye! Yes, it was this! One of his eyes resembled that of a vulture—a pale blue eye with a film over it. Whenever it fell upon me my blood ran cold, and so by degrees, very gradually, I made up my mind to take the life of the old man, and thus rid myself of the eye for ever.

King Lear, by William Shakespeare

OSWALD: Why dost thou use me thus? I know thee not.

KENT: Fellow, I know thee.

OSWALD: What dost thou know me for?

KENT: A knave; a rascal; an eater of broken meats; a base, proud, shallow, beggarly, three-suited, hundred-pound, filthy, worsted-stocking knave; a lily-livered, action-taking whoreson, glass-gazing, superserviceable, finical rogue; one-trunk-inheriting slave; one that wouldst be a bawd, in way of good service, and art nothing but the composition of a knave, beggar, coward, pander, and the son and heir of a mongrel bitch: one whom I will beat into clamorous whining, if thou deniest the least syllable of thy addition.

OSWALD: Why what a monstrous fellow art thou, thus to rail on one that is neither known of thee nor knows thee!

KENT: What a brazen-faced varlet art thou, to deny thou knowest me! It is two days ago since I tripped up thy heels, and beat thee before the king? Draw, you rogue: for though it be night, yet the moon shines; I'll make a sop o' the moonshine of you: draw, you cullionly barbermonger, draw.

Frankenstein, by Mary Shelley

The words induced me to turn towards myself. I learned that the possession most esteemed by your fellow-creatures were high and unsullied decent united with riches. A man might be respected with only one of these acquisitions; but without either he was considered, except in very rare instances, as a vagabond and a slave, doomed to waste his powers for the profit of the chosen few. And what was I? Of my creation and creator I was absolutely ignorant; but I knew that I possessed no money, no friends, no kind of property. I was, besides, endowed with a figure hideously deformed and loathsome; I was not even of the same nature as man. I was more agile than they, and could subsist upon coarser diet; I bore the extremes of heat and cold with less injury to my frame; my stature far exceeded theirs. When I looked around, I saw and heard of none like me. Was I then a monster, a blot upon the earth, from which all men fled, and whom all men disowned?

The Strange Case of Dr. Jekyll and Mr. Hyde, by Robert Louis Stevenson

It was this way. I came into the theatre from the garden. It seems he had slipped out to look for this drug or whatever it is; for the cabinet door was open, and there he was at the far end of the room digging among the crate. He looked up when I came in, gave a kind of cry, and whipped upstairs into the cabinet. It was but for one minute that I saw him, but the air stood upon my head like quills. Sir, if that was my master, why had he a mask upon his face? If it was my master, why did he cry out like a rat, and run from me?

Treasure Island, by Robert Louis Stevenson

"Who are you?" I asked.

"Ben Gunn," he answered, and his voice sounded hoarse and awkward, like a rusty lock. "I'm poor Ben Gunn, I am; and I haven't spoke with a Christian these three years."

I could now see that he was a white man like myself, and that his features were even pleasing. His skin, wherever it was exposed, was burnt by the sun; even his lips were black; and his fair eyes looked quite startling in so dark a face. Of all the beggarmen that I had seen or fancied, he was the chief for raggedness. . . . About his waist he wore an old brass-buckled leather belt, which was the thing solid in his whole accoutrement.

"Three years!" I cried. "Were you shipwrecked?"

"Nay, mate," said he—"marooned." . . .

"Marooned three years agone," he continued, "and lived on goats since then, and berries, and oysters. Wherever a man is, says I, a man can do for himself. But, mate, my heart is sore for Christian diet. You mightn't happen to have a piece of cheese about you, now? No? Well, many's the long night I've dreamed of cheese—toasted, mostly—and woke up again, and here I were."

Dracula, by Bram Stoker

When Lucy, I call the thing that was before us Lucy because it bore her shape, saw us she drew back with an angry snarl, such as a cat gives when taken unawares, then her eyes ranged over us. Lucy's eyes in form and color, but Lucy's eyes unclean and full of hell fire, instead of the pure gentle orbs we knew. At the moment the remnant of my love passed into hate and loathing. Had she then to be killed, I could have done it with savage delight. As she looked, her eyes blazed with unholy light, and the face became wreathed with a voluptuous smile. Oh, God, how it made me shudder to see it! With a careless motion, she flung to the ground, callous as a devil, the child that up to now she had clutched strenuously to her breast growling over it as a dog growls over a bone.

Vanity Fair, by William Makepeace Thackeray

Mrs. Rawdon Crawley's début was, on the contrary, very brilliant. She arrived very late. Her face was radiant; her dress perfection. In the midst of the great persons assembled, and the eye-glasses directed to her, Rebecca seemed to be as cool and collected as when she used to marshal Miss Pinkerton's little girls to church. Numbers of the men she knew already, and the dandies thronged round her. As for the ladies, it was whispered among them that Rawdon had run away with her from out of a convent, and that she was a relation of the Montmorency family. She spoke French so perfectly that there might be some truth in this report, and it was agreed that her manners were fine, and her air *distingué*. Fifty would-be partners thronged round her at once, and pressed to have the honour to dance with her. . . . She vowed that it was a delightful ball; that there was everybody that every one knew, and only a very few nobodies in the whole room.

The Adventures of Tom Sawyer, by Mark Twain

Shortly Tom came upon the juvenile pariah of the village, Huckleberry Finn, son of the town drunkard. Huckleberry was cordially hated and dreaded by all the mothers of the town, because he was idle and lawless and vulgar and bad—and because all their children admired him so, and delighted in his forbidden society, and wished they dared to be like him. Tom was like the rest of the respectable boys, in that he envied Huckleberry his gaudy outcast condition, and was under strict orders not to play with him. So he played with him every time he got a chance. . . .

Huckleberry came and went, at his own free will. He slept on doorsteps in fine weather and in empty hogsheads in wet; he did not have to go to school or to church, or call any being master or obey anybody; he could go fishing or swimming when and where he chose, and stay as long as it suited him; nobody forbade him to fight; he could sit up as late as he pleased; he was always the first boy that went barefoot in the spring and the last to resume leather in the fall; he never had to wash, nor put on clean clothes; he could swear wonderfully. In a word, everything that goes to make life precious that boy had. So thought every harassed, hampered, respectable boy in St. Petersburg.

The Picture of Dorian Gray, by Oscar Wilde

Yet it was watching him, with its beautiful marred face and its cruel smile. Its bright hair gleamed in the early sunlight. Its blue eyes met his own. A sense of infinite pity, not for himself, but for the painted image of himself, came over him. It had altered already, and would alter more. Its gold would wither into grey. Its red and white roses would die. For every sin that he committed, a stain would fleck and wreck its fairness. But he would not sin. The picture, changed or unchanged, would be to him the visible emblem of conscience. He would resist temptation. He would not see Lord Henry any more—would not, at any rate, listen to those subtle poisonous theories that in Basil Hallward's garden had first stirred within him the passion for impossible things.

20,000 Leagues Under the Sea, by Jules Verne

Before my eyes was a horrible monster worthy to figure in the legends of the marvelous. It was an immense cuttlefish, being eight yards long. It swam crossways in the direction of the Nautilus with great speed, watching us with its enormous staring green eyes. Its eight arms, or rather feet, fixed to its head, that have given the name of cephalopod to these animals, were twice as long as its body, and were twisted like the furies' hair. One could see the 250 air-holes on the inner side of the tentacles. The monster's mouth, a horned beak like a parrot's, opened and shut vertically. Its tongue, a horned substance, furnished with several rows of pointed teeth, came out quivering from this veritable pair of shears. What a freak of nature, a bird's beak on a mollusk! Its spindle-like body formed a fleshy mass that might weigh 4,000 to 5,000 lbs. . . . I overcame the horror that inspired me, and, taking a pencil, began to draw it.

"Brown Penny," by William Butler Yeats

I WHISPERED, 'I am too young,'
And then, 'I am old enough';
Wherefore I threw a penny
To find out if I might love.
'Go and love, go and love, young man,
If the lady be young and fair.'
Ah, penny, brown penny, brown penny,
I am looped in the loops of her hair.
O love is the crooked thing,
There is nobody wise enough
To find out all that is in it,
For he would be thinking of love
Till the stars had run away
And the shadows eaten the moon.
Ah, penny, brown penny, brown penny,
One cannot begin it too soon.